Cooking
INN
Style

A Bed & Breakfast Guide
& Bed & Breakfast Recipe Cookbook

By Sonnie Imes
and
The Bed & Breakfast Innkeepers
of Northern California

ISBN # 0-9617881-0-0

This cookbook is dedicated to all of the wonderful inn guests who have made bed and breakfast a way of travelling.

In our spirit of hospitality we offer you these recipes. Happy cooking!

Special thanks to Rosalie Hope and Susan Clow, the primary "movers and shakers" of this book— and to all the innkeepers who so willingly cooperated by taking time out of their busy inn-keeping schedules to share their fabulous recipes.

With much appreciation to Sonnie Imes for the many hours of guiding, editing and mothering "COOKING INN STYLE."

TABLE OF CONTENTS
Bed and Breakfast Inns
Of Northern California

GOLD COUNTRY INNS

- American River Inn
- Baretta Gardens Inn
- Botto Country Inn
- Chichester House
- City Hotel
- Feather Bed
- Foxes
- Gate House Inn
- Hanford House
- The Heirloom
- Murphy's Inn
- Nancy & Bob's
- Oak Hill Ranch
- Red Castle Inn
- White Sulphur Springs Ranch

1

American River Inn

Main at Orleans Street • Georgetown, California 95634
(916) 333-4499

This restored miners' boarding house features Victorian antiques, gardens, a mountain stream pool with jacuzzi and a dove aviary. Breakfast is served in the morning, local wines and treats in the evening. Off-street parking. Handicapped facilities.

3

Lemon Date Pecan Muffins

½ c. brown sugar
6 tbsp. unsalted butter
5 tbsp. lemon juice
¼ c. honey
½ c. sour cream
1 egg
1 tbsp. grated lemon peel
1¾ c. flour
1½ tsp. baking powder
½ tsp. baking soda
¾ tsp. salt
1 c chopped dates
1 c. chopped pecans
¼ c. hot water

Preheat oven to 400° F.

Cook brown sugar, butter, lemon juice and honey in saucepan until hot. Whisk sour cream, egg, lemon peel in bowl. Whisk in brown sugar mixture.

Combine flour, baking powder, baking soda, and salt in another bowl. Add to liquid ingredients and stir. Add dates and pecans and hot water and stir until blended.

Bake 20 minutes in 14 buttered muffin cups.

Serves 7

Barretta Gardens Inn

700 S. Barretta St. • Sonora, California 95370
(209) 532-6039

Come share the beauty of old-fashioned gardens and the comforts of our turn-of-the-century inn. Enjoy homemade breakfast on the front porch or indoors and then on to explore downtown Sonora and other nearby historical areas.

Strata

12 slices white bread or French bread, crust removed
½ lb. grated cheese, jack and/or cheddar
1 c. diced ham
6 eggs
3 c. milk
Salt and pepper to taste

Butter or spray 9x13 pyrex dish, place 6 slices of bread on bottom of dish. Sprinkle half of cheese and diced ham over bread. Place other 6 slices of bread and sprinkle with remaining ham and cheese. Beat eggs, add milk and seasonings, pour over bread and cheese. Let set in refrigerator for 24 hours. Bake uncovered at 350° for one hour or until knife comes out clean. Vary this recipe by adding sliced mushrooms or diced zucchini. Diced Ortegas' green chiles can be used and served with a mild salsa (warmed) to pour over. The variations are many. When adding fresh vegetables decrease the milk a little as the vegetables contain a lot of moisture.

Take it out of the refrigerator first thing in the morning. Place it in the oven one hour and 15 minutes before you plan to serve. It cuts better if you let it sit awhile.

Kolaczki

½ lb. margarine
1 8-oz. package cream cheese
2½ c. white flour
You can use preserves of your choice for filling, or a canned
    fruit pastry filling
Confectioner's sugar

Bring margarine and cream cheese to room temperature and
knead in flour. Work to fine texture. Put in refrigerator for at least
2 hours or overnight. Cut a small piece of dough at a time and roll
out thin and cut into squares approximately 2½ inches each side.
Put a teaspoon of preserves in middle, fold four corners and pinch
closed. Bake on ungreased cookie sheet in 350° oven for approximately 20 minutes. Kolaczkis should be a light brown. Remove,
sprinkle with confectioner's sugar.

Onion Bread

1 c. minced green onions
1 c. grated parmesan cheese
1 c. mayonnaise
English muffins, French bread or any other kind of bread

Onions should be chopped very small. Add cheese and mayonnaise and blend to a creamy consistency. Spread on English muffins, French bread or any bread of your choice. Heat under the broiler just until they get that light, golden brown. Wonderful! Can be prepared in smaller quantities as long as the portions are kept equal.

Wonder Cake

Mocha flavor
1 package chocolate or devil's food cake mix
4 eggs
½ c. cooking oil
1 c. water
1 package (3½ ounces) chocolate instant pudding mix
2 tbsp. instant coffee powder
1 tsp. vanilla extract

Turn all ingredients into the large bowl of an electric mixer. Using a rubber spatula to push ingredients into mixer blades, mix at low speed until ingredients are well blended. Beat at medium speed four minutes. Bake in a 10-inch tube pan or a bundt pan. Prepare pan by buttering thoroughly, then shake some granulated sugar inside the pan to coat all sides. This gives your cake a nice little crust. Bake in a preheated 350° oven for 45 to 55 minutes, or until the cake tests done with a toothpick or cake tester. Each cake makes about 16 servings.

The best feature about this cake is the many combinations you can create. Vary the type of cake mix and the pudding flavor. You can substitute a liqueur for a portion of the water, as long as the liquids equal one cup. Imagine an Amaretto flavored cake with slivered almonds, yum. Add nuts, mashed fruit in season—the sky is the limit!

The Botto Country Inn

11 Sutter Hill Road • Sutter Creek, California 95635
(209) 267-5519

An 1860 farmhouse in a country setting across from the Central Eureka Mine. Next door is a rock building built in 1871 which once housed the Botto Saloon. While relaxing on the porch you can almost hear the chatter of the miners.

Brown Potatoes

Potatoes
Olive oil
Soy sauce
Onion powder
Pepper
Italian seasoning

Bake as many potatoes as you need (1 per person), cut in half lengthwise, leaving skin on. Place in baking pan, oiled with olive oil, skin side down. Sprinkle with soy sauce until brown and about ½ tsp. olive oil on each potato.

For more flavor, sprinkle with onion, pepper, and Italian seasoning.

Bake for 30 minutes in a 350° oven. These potatoes can be kept warm until ready to be served. A great potato for breakfast, brunch or dinner.

Sherry Currant Orange Sauce

1 c. orange juice
½ c. sherry
½ c. currants
½ tsp. cinnamon
¼ tsp. cloves
1 apple (red or green) sliced thin
1 tsp. or less cornstarch
Zest of ½ orange

Place first six ingredients in saucepan. Stir and blend. Let simmer with lid on for 10 minutes. Mix cornstarch with a little water and thicken sauce to desired thickness.

Place sausage or ham on platter. Pour sauce over and garnish with orange zest.

Excellent over sausages of any kind and smoked ham.

Baked Onions in Balsamic Vinegar

Yellow onion
Balsamic vinegar
Brown sugar

Wash onions. Cut in half, leaving skins on. Place in baking pan, cut side up.

On each onion put 1 tbsp. vinegar and 1 tsp. brown sugar. Cover with foil. Bake 350° for about 1½ hours.

The Chichester House

890 Spring Street • Placerville, California 95667
(916) 626-1882

Our 1892 Victorian offers comfortable elegance. Half-baths in three cozy guestrooms. Large parlor and library, many family treasures, winter fireplaces, summer air-conditioning. Very special breakfasts. Downtown Placerville.

15

Two Hour Rolls

1 pint scalded milk
¼ c. margarine
1½ tsp. salt
Two beaten eggs
¼ c. sugar
1½ cakes yeast
5 c. flour more or less

Scald milk, add margarine until melted and add salt. Set aside to cool. Beat eggs in large bowl. In small bowl, mix sugar and yeast until it liquifies. Add this to egg mixture. Add cooled milk mixture. Add 3 cups flour and mix well. Stir in additional flour until batter makes a soft, not sticky dough. Let rise 1 hour. On floured board make into bread rolls, cinnamon rolls or coffee rings. Let rise 45 minutes and bake in 400°F. oven. This dough may be kept in refrigerator for about 5 days and used as needed. (As brown and serve it works well. Not for loaves.) For cinnamon rolls or coffee rings, lightly butter rolled out dough. Add cinnamon, raisins and nuts.

(Use half the dough at a time.) Roll up and slice into nine cinnamon rolls for each half of dough. For coffee rings, form a ring in center of greased baking sheet. With kitchen shears cut to within 1 inch of center of dough making 8 to 10 even cuts. With hands, take each section and turn it slightly fanning out the dough into a pretty ring. A simple glaze may be used over all when cooled.

Serves 2 dozen rolls, 1½ dozen cinnamon rolls or 2 coffee rings.

Pears in Wine

1½ c. unsweetened grape juice
2 c. white wine
¾ c. sugar
Zest from half a medium lemon
6 slightly under ripe pears, peeled and cored
½ tsp. vanilla

In stainless or similar pan, combine grape juice, wine, sugar and lemon zest. Bring to boil and turn heat down to simmer, cook for 10 minutes. Place pears which have been peeled and cored in liquid and simmer 20 to 30 minutes until pears are tender but still firm. Cool slightly and add vanilla. Serve any temperature. (They look beautiful in a stemmed goblet.)

Serves 6

Tea Time Anise Toast

2 eggs
⅔ c. sugar
1 tsp. crushed anise seed
1 c. flour

Preheat oven to 375°F.

Grease and flour 8x4x2 loaf pan.

Beat eggs and sugar. Add crushed anise seed and gradually add flour. Pour into prepared pan. Bake about 20 minutes or until toothpick inserted comes out clean. Remove loaf from pan and cool on rack. Slice into 12 even slices. Bake slices on greased baking sheet for about 5 minutes or until bottom of slices are browned. Turn over and repeat on other side. Cool. (Toasting should be done in 450°F. oven.)

Yields 12 slices

City Hotel

Box 1870, Main Street • Columbia, California 95310
(209) 532-1479

Built in 1856 and located in a state-preserved, historic Gold Rush town, the City Hotel offers the comfort of an elegantly appointed bed and breakfast inn together with an intimate French restaurant and authentic saloon.

19

Cream of Mushroom with Pimento Puree

1 leek, washed and sliced
2 tbsp. butter
1 lb. mushrooms, washed
1 medium baker's potato, washed, peeled and cubed
3 quarts white stock or beef consomme
1 strip of bacon, cooked
Cream
Salt and white pepper
Butter
Tabasco

Saute leek in butter until transparent, being careful not to burn the butter or leek. Put in stock pot or large sauce pan, add the cooked leek, mushrooms, potato and stock. The stock should lightly cover the potatoes about one inch. Add the bacon, bring to a boil, covered, and simmer until the potatoes are well cooked. Pour in a blender and blend saving some of the liquid, in case the puree is too thick. Return the mushroom puree to sauce pan and add cream, salt, pepper, butter and tabasco to attain the right texture and taste. Add saved stock if soup is too thick. Strain and serve with pimento puree. The soup should be on the thick side to "hold up" the pimento puree. The pimento puree is canned pimentos blended and strained without the juice from the can.

Croustade de Homard
Au Whiskey
(Lobster in Pastry Shell)

2 c. whiskey
3 c. whipping cream
2 lbs. lobster tail meat cut into 1" cubes
3 tbs. cool butter
Salt and white pepper

Heat whiskey in saute pan. Add cream and reduce by one-half. Add lobster meat, continue reducing until thickened, fold in butter, season and divide among Brioches (recipe follows).

Pastry Shells (Brioches)

Puff pastry (buy or make) rolled out to 10"x15". Cut into 8 equal pieces and brushed with egg wash. Cut into 4 of the pieces a rectangle ½ inch in from edge and stack cut ones onto the uncut ones. Bake at 425°F., making large brioches. When cool, cut off top, save and hollow out insides for lobster.

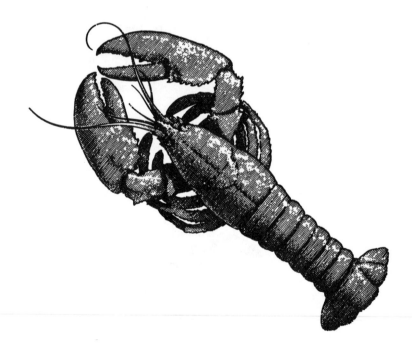

Shrimp Shirred Eggs

SHRIMP CREAM SAUCE:
2 tbs. clarified butter
1 large shallot, chopped
1 c. brut champagne
1½ lb. frozen or fresh shrimp
3 c. whipping cream
¼ c. unsalted butter

Heat butter in large skillet, saute chopped shallots lightly. Add champagne and reduce by one-half. Add shrimp and cook gently for 2 to 3 minutes, remove with slotted spoon and keep warm. Increase heat and reduce juices to a thin glaze. Blend in cream to sauce pan and simmer until mixture thickens, about 20 to 30 minutes. Remove from heat and whisk in butter and cooked shrimp. Taste and season and pour over shirred eggs. Garnish with olive rounds.

SHIRRED EGGS:
8 large eggs

Butter a shallow oven proof casserole dish large enough to hold 8 eggs, lightly with a brush. Crack eggs in dish and dot each yolk with oil or clarified butter. Bake uncovered in oven at 350°F. until yolks are set.

Serves 4

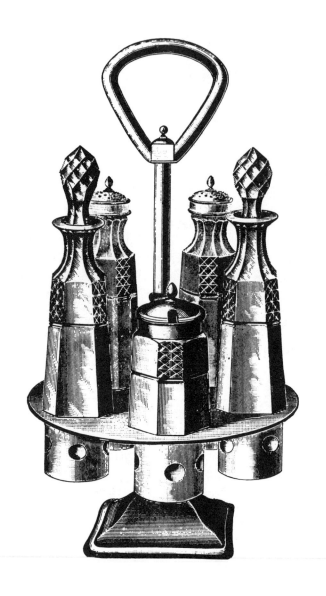

BED AND BREAKFAST

542 Jackson Street (Box 3200) • Quincy, California 95971
(916) 283-0102

Country Victorian inn, five charmingly decorated rooms with antiques, private baths, some with clawfoot tubs, located in a pristine wilderness area of the Plumas National Forest. Located on the historic Heritage Walk adjacent to downtown Quincy.

25

Chocolate Almond Zucchini Bread

3 c. sifted flour
2 c. sugar
1¼ tsp. baking powder
1 tsp. salt
1 tsp. cinnamon
1 c. chopped almonds
1 c. oil
1 tsp. vanilla
3 eggs
2 1-ounce squares unsweetened chocolate (melted)
2 c. zucchini, shredded

Into a large bowl sift together first 5 ingredients. Stir in almonds.
In medium bowl mix oil, vanilla, eggs, and chocolate until well
blended. Stir in zucchini. Then stir zucchini mixture into dry
ingredients, just until moistened. Pour into greased loaf pan. Bake
350° 1 hour 30 minutes.

Serves 8

26

Bran Muffins

2 c. boiling water
6 c. whole bran cereal
3 c. sugar
1 c. shortening
3 c. raisins
1 qt. buttermilk
4 eggs
5 c. sifted flour
1 tsp. salt
5 tsp. baking soda

Pour boiling water over 2 cups cereal, set aside. Cream sugar, shortening, raisins, buttermilk and eggs together. Fold flour, salt, baking soda, and remaining cereal into creamed mixture. Add soaked cereal to batter, mix only until dry ingredients are moistened. (Can store in refrigerator up to 6 weeks.) Spoon into greased muffin tins, ⅔ full. Bake at 400° for 18-20 minutes.

Yields 18 muffins

The Foxes

77 Main Street, Box 159 • Sutter Creek, California 95685
(209) 267-5882

An 1857 inn with six suites and private baths, queen beds. Bountiful breakfast served to each on gleaming silver service. Hospitality is number one. Peter and Min Fox, Innkeeper.

29

Swiss Eggs

4 eggs
2 tbsp. melted butter
½ c. cream
½ tsp. pepper
A few grains cayenne
2 tbsp. grated cheddar cheese
4 English muffins, halved and toasted
6 slices crisp bacon

Slide eggs into butter and cream in a skillet. Sprinkle with pepper and cayenne. Heat and when whites begin to set, sprinkle with cheese. Finish cooking and serve on muffin halves with some of the hot cream and butter. Place crisp bacon on the side. Garnish with a slice of fresh fruit in season and a sprig of fresh herb.

Serves 2, with healthy appetites

Fresh Strawberry Butter

1 c. fresh strawberries, cranberries or raspberries
¾ c. confectioner's sugar
1 stick unsalted butter (4 oz.) at room temperature, cut into
    4 pieces

Using a food processor fitted with a steel knife, process berries until pureed, stopping machine once to scrape down sides of bowl. Add sugar and butter and process 2 or 3 minutes or until smooth, fluffy and bright pink. Spoon into a 1½ c. crock or jar, wrap airtight and refrigerate. Let the mixture soften at room temperature for 2 hours before serving. Do not melt in microwave oven. Butter freezes beautifully. Serve with your favorite French toast, pancakes or waffles. Imagine how wonderful the cranberry butter will be with hot yeast muffins at either Thanksgiving or Christmas!

Bon Appetit!

Serves 6 to 8

Fresh Apple Coffee Cake

1 c. all purpose flour
½ tsp. salt
1 tbsp. soda
2 c. cored, peeled, diced sweet apple
1 egg
¼ c. salad oil
1 c. sugar
1 tsp. ground cinnamon
¼ tsp. ground nutmeg
¾ c. nuts (chopped coarsely)

Sift flour, salt and soda together; set aside. Place apple in a medium sized bowl. Break egg over apples. Add oil, sugar, cinnamon, nutmeg and nuts; blend thoroughly. Stir dry mixture into apple mixture just until flour is moist (seems dry). Spread in greased 8 inch square baking pan. Bake in 350° oven for 40-45 minutes or until a wooden toothpick inserted in center comes out clean. Let stand in pan for 10 minutes before turning out on a wire rack.

Serves 9

Gate House Inn

1330 Jackson Gate Road • Jackson, California 95642
(209) 223-3500

A stately Victorian with spacious gardens, marble fireplaces, oak parquet floors, crystal chandeliers, and a large antique clock collection. Swimming pool in summer. A relaxing experience in the country. Five rooms with private baths. Frank and Ursel Walker, Innkeepers.

Festive Pancakes

1 c. all-purpose flour
1 tsp. baking powder
½ tsp. baking soda
1 tbsp. sugar
½ tsp. salt
2 eggs (slightly beaten)
2 tbsp. melted butter
1 c. buttermilk
1 large apple, grated
¼ c. walnuts
¼ c. raisins
½ tsp. cinnamon

Mix dry ingredients together in a bowl. Add eggs, butter and buttermilk. Stir until batter is smooth. Let batter rest 5 minutes. For each pancake use about ¼ cup batter. Pour batter onto hot greased griddle or fry pan. Cook until top is full of bubbles and underside is golden brown. Turn and cook until golden brown on other side. Garnish with apples, walnuts, raisins and cinnamon.

Makes 10 pancakes

Fresh Strawberry Butter

1 cube butter, room temperature
1½ c. powdered sugar
½ tsp. vanilla
1 c. strawberries (quartered, then sliced)

Cream butter and add powdered sugar. Beat until smooth. Add vanilla. Add strawberries. Mix well. Wonderful over warm croissants.

Serves 8-10

Marinated Mushroom Dressing

1½ lbs. mushrooms, sliced
1 c. olive oil (must be olive oil)
8 tbsp. red wine vinegar
2 tsp. salt
1 tsp. pepper
4 cloves garlic, chopped fine
1 tsp. Accent

Combine all ingredients. Marinate for 3 days in refrigerator. Stir frequently. Remove from refrigerator several hours before serving. Serve over mixed salad.

The Hanford House

Hwy. 49 (Box 847) • Sutter Creek, California 95685
(209) 267-0747

Nine spacious rooms blending the elegance of a gracious past with all the comforts of today. Queen-size beds, private baths, air conditioning and handicapped accessible. Large deck and patio. Hearty continental breakfast in your room.

37

Lemon Cake

6 tbsp. butter or margarine
1 c. sugar
2 beaten eggs
1 grated rind of lemon
1½ c. flour
½ tsp. salt
½ tsp. baking powder
½ c. milk
½ c. chopped walnuts (optional)

TOPPING:

½ c. sugar
Juice of one lemon

Cream together butter and sugar. Beat in the 2 eggs and grated rind of one lemon. Sift together the flour, salt and baking powder. Add milk to egg mixture. Stir in nuts.

Pour into well-greased loaf pan. Bake at 350° 40-50 minutes. Test with toothpick for doneness. Remove from oven. Cool in pan 10 minutes. Punch holes with fork on top of cake. Combine sugar and lemon juice. Pour *slowly* over cake. Cool completely in pan before removing.

Freezes beautifully! Keeps well, wrapped in foil in refrigerator. This is really best served cold and sliced thinly with tea in the afternoon! Enjoy!

Applesauce Cake

½ c. butter or margarine
¾ c. granulated sugar
1 beaten egg
2 c. sifted flour
½ tsp. salt
1 tsp. baking soda
1 tsp. baking powder
1 tsp. cinnamon
¼ tsp. powdered cloves
1 tsp. nutmeg
1 c. chopped walnuts
½ c. raisins (optional)
1 c. thick sweetened applesauce (make your own and use the
    best apples!)

Cream butter until fluffy. Gradually add sugar, continuing to cream butter until well blended and light. Add egg. Sift together flour, salt, soda, baking powder, cinnamon, cloves and nutmeg. Add nuts (and raisins) to dry ingredients.

Heat applesauce to boiling point. Add to sugar-butter mixture alternately with flour mixture. Pour into greased loaf pan (9"x5"x3"). Bake 350° for 55-60 minutes. Test with toothpick.

Eggs Elegante

1 c. (or more) shredded jack cheese
16 Jones' sausages (cooked)
8 eggs (uncooked)
16 cherry tomatoes
Green onions (chopped)
Salt, pepper, Fines Herbes
Sherry

Spray 4 individual Ramekins with vegetable spray. Spread bottom of each with one-fourth of the jack cheese. Circle the inside of ramekins with 4 cooked sausages each. Gently break 2 eggs in center of each, keeping yolks intact. Cut tomatoes in half and circle 4 around edges in between sausages. Sprinkle with green onions, salt, pepper, Fine herbes. Splash with sherry. Bake until eggs are set (according to individual taste) in 350° oven.

Serves 4

The Heirloom
Circa 1863

214 Shakeley Lane • Ione, California 95640
(209) 274-4468

Down a country lane to an expansive garden setting—a petite colonial mansion, circa 1863—verandas, fireplaces, heirloom antiques, French country breakfast, comfort, gracious hospitality. Melisande Hubbs and Patricia Cross, Innkeepers.

Neptune Pie (Quiche)

1 Pie shell
8 oz. crabmeat, shrimp or other seafood
6 slices bacon (cooked crisp and crumbled)
1 tbsp. cornstarch
2 c. Half and Half
4 eggs
½ tsp. salt
¼ tsp. nutmeg
1 tbsp. onion flakes
1 tbsp. fresh basil
2 c. Swiss cheese

Bake pie shell 10 minutes at 400°. Cool and fill shell evenly with seafood and bacon. Beat together cornstarch, Half and Half, eggs, salt, nutmeg, onion flakes, and basil. Pour in shell (over seafood and bacon). Cover with Swiss cheese. Bake at 375° for 40 minutes.

Serves 8

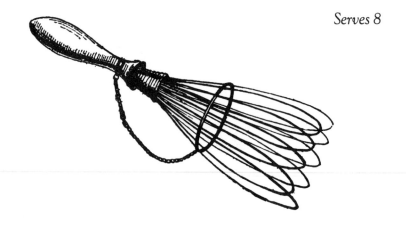

Georgia Nut Bread

1½ c. dates
1½ c. sugar
2 tbsp. butter
1 tsp. salt
1 egg
2¾ c. flour
1 tsp. cream of tartar
1 tsp. soda
½ tsp. vanilla
1 c. chopped nuts

Chop (cut up) dates, plumped first by covering with 1½ cups boiling water. Add sugar, butter and salt. Set aside to cool. Add egg (well beaten). Add remaining dry ingredients, vanilla and nuts. Bake in loaf pan at 350° for 1 hour.

Serves 12

Melon-Mint Medley

4 c. fresh melon balls
⅔ c. sugar
⅓ c. lemon juice
2 tbsp. finely chopped mint

Combine all ingredients. Mix lightly. Chill 3-4 hours or overnight.

Serves 6

318 Neal Street • Grass Valley, California 95945
(916) 273-6873

In 1866 Murphy's Inn was originally built as the personal estate of one of the Mother Lode's famous gold barons, Edward Coleman. Today Murphy's Inn offers the splendor and beauty of the Victorian era to the discriminating traveler.

Marc's Mexican Pie

12 corn tortillas
Melted butter or oil
8 oz. softened cream cheese
48 oz. (6 cups) refried beans
12 eggs, poached
Grated cheddar cheese
Sour cream
Guacamole
Fresh salsa (recipe follows)
Lettuce, shredded
Black olives

Saute tortillas in butter or oil. Remove from heat and spread with thin layer of cream cheese. Top with ½ cup hot refried beans. Place poached egg on beans and sprinkle with cheddar cheese. Serve with side bowls of sour cream, guacamole, and fresh salsa (recipe follows). Garnish with shredded lettuce and black olives.

Serves 12

Fresh Salsa

10 oz. Hunt's tomato sauce
1 finely chopped yellow onion
2 finely chopped green onions
1 diced tomato
1 tbsp. lemon juice
1 tbsp. fresh cilantro, chopped
1 tsp. salt
1 tsp. fresh diced or powdered garlic
½ bell pepper, diced (optional)

Blend all ingredients well. Chill. (DO NOT COOK.) Salsa will keep in refrigerator for approximately 2 weeks.

Belgian Waffles

4 eggs, separated
2 c. milk
½ c. melted butter
1 tsp. vanilla
2 c. all-purpose flour
2 tsp. baking powder
1 tsp. baking soda
1 tbsp. sugar
½ tsp. salt
Fresh fruit and maple syrup or cherry sauce (recipe follows)
Sweetened whipped cream

Beat the egg yolks. Beat in the milk, melted butter and vanilla.
Combine and sift together the flour, baking powder, soda, sugar
and salt into the egg-milk mixture. Beat well. Beat the egg whites
in a separate bowl until stiff. Carefully fold into the batter. Bake
in a Belgian waffle iron 3 to 4 minutes. Top with fresh fruit and
maple syrup or cherry sauce and whipped cream.

Serves 8-10

Cherry Sauce

¼ c. sugar
2 tsp. cornstarch
1/8 tsp. cinnamon
½ c. orange juice
2 c. pitted and halved fresh sweet cherries
1 tsp. grated orange peel

Combine the sugar, cornstarch and cinnamon. Add the orange juice, cherries and peel. Bring to a boil over medium-high heat. Boil until thickened.

Nancy & Bob's
9 Eureka Street Inn

P.O. Box 386 • Sutter Creek, California 95685
(209) 267-0342

Enjoy warm friendly hospitality amidst graciousness and charm of yesteryear in a beautiful 1916 California bungalow replete in rich woods, antiques, and guest rooms decorated in mode of the past. Queen-sized beds. Private baths. Air conditioned. Free brochure.

Jenny's Eggs

7 slices sandwich bread (cubed)
½ lb. Velveeta cheese
1 cube butter
1 cube margarine
4 eggs beaten
2 c. milk

Place bread cubes in dish. Melt cheese, butter and margarine.
Pour over bread. Mix eggs and milk. Pour over bread and cheese.
Refrigerate overnight. Place in oven and turn on at 300° in 7"x12"
Pyrex dish for 45 minutes to 1 hour.

Serves 10

Oak Hill Ranch
BED & BREAKFAST

18550 Connally Ln., Box 307 • Tuolumne, California 95379
(209) 928-4717

For a "Perfect Sojourn into the Past," Oak Hill Ranch is the perfect answer for an extraordinary overnight stay in a country Victorian or private cottage on 56 acres at 3,000 elevation, close to summer/winter resorts and Yosemite National Park. Full gourmet breakfasts and matchless hospitality.

Crepes Normandie

CREPES:
1 egg
Dash of salt
½ c. and 1 tbsp. flour
1 tsp. vegetable oil
⅔ c. milk

FILLING:
1 c. Mott's brand chunky applesauce
½ c. raisins, soaked for ½ hour in 2 tbsp. brandy
Dash cinnamon
Dash cardamon
Walnuts, chopped somewhat fine

DRESSING:
Sour cream
Brown sugar
Blueberries or blackberries
Chopped walnuts

Beat all crepe ingredients together to a thin liquid-like consistency. Bake in crepe pan in medium heat until barely brown.

Mix together all filling ingredients.

Mix sour cream and brown sugar. Add berries separately on top and more coarsely chopped walnuts. Each crepe takes about two serving spoons of applesauce filling. Bake the filled crepes in pan 15 minutes in oven at 350°. *Afterwards*, place dressing on top. Serve hot. Garnish plate with fresh fruit in season and with sausages or bacon. Add parsley.

Serves 2

Sandy's Scrumptious Spuds

¼ cube butter
1 tbsp. corn oil
Dash onion flakes
Dash parsley flakes
Season with garlic salt
1 clove garlic (squeeze in garlic press)
1 medium russet potato (slice into 3/8" thick slices)
1 tbsp. water

Use cast iron covered Grizwold skillet. Melt butter in skillet. Add corn oil, onion flakes, parsley flakes, garlic salt and squeezed garlic clove. Mix thoroughly. Place sliced potatoes over mixture. Add water. Cook on *low heat* with skillet covered. After 20 minutes or so, turn potato slices over. Continue cooking another 20 minutes. If more water is needed add another tablespoon. Serve hot. This goes well with omelets.

Cup 'O Gold & Sausage

Prepare basic recipe for crepes
8 oz. bulk pork sausage or 10 links of "brown 'n serve" links
½ c. chopped green bell pepper
½ c. chopped white onion
¼ c. chopped pimento
6 eggs
¼ c. milk
1 tsp. salt
¼ tsp. garlic powder
½ pint sour cream
¼ c. minced chives
2 drops Tabasco pepper sauce (optional)

Preheat oven to 375°. Grease standard sized muffin tin. Make six crepes, about 5" diameter, and place into muffin tin. Ruffle edges. **Prepare sausage mix:** Mash sausage into bits. Combine sausage with bell pepper, onion and pimento in skillet and cook over medium heat until sausage turns lightly browned. **Prepare egg mix:** Lightly beat eggs with milk, salt and garlic powder until blended. **Assemble:** Place about three tablespoons full of sausage mix into crepe cups. Pour three tablespoons full of egg mix over the sausage. Bake 25 minutes. Test with knife until knife comes out clean. Let set for five minutes. Remove from muffin tin. Top cups with sour cream and chives. *Recommend* two crepes per person, in which case *double* the above recipe for six persons. If more highly seasoned effect is desired, add 2 drops Tabasco pepper sauce blended in with the sausage mix. Garnish plate with fresh fruits of the season, plus parsley or watercress. Hot breads may be served on the side.

Serves 3

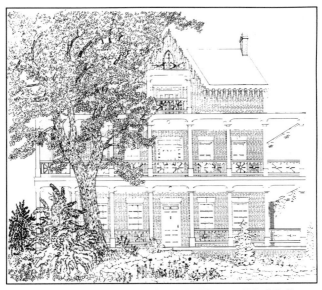

· RED · CASTLE · INN ·

109 Prospect Street • Nevada City, California 95959
(916) 265-5135

In the main parlour at the Red Castle tea is served each afternoon, as guests arrive, as a respite from the day's journey. Our two most often requested recipes from the tea table follow.

57

Petticoat Tails

1 c. butter, softened
2½ c. sifted flour
6 tbsp. sugar

Blend all ingredients together until the dough holds its shape. Press into a 9" round cake pan and score into 16 wedges. Bake at 300° 30-40 minutes or until slightly colored at the edge. Cool in the pan. Slice along scored lines before completely cooled. Store air tight.

Serves 16.

Raw Apple Cake

4 c. chopped, peeled apples
2 c. sugar
½ c. oil
1 tsp. vanilla
2 beaten eggs
1 c. chopped walnuts
1 c. raisins

2 c. flour
1 tsp. salt
1 tsp. baking powder
2 tsp. cinnamon
½ tsp. cloves
½ tsp. nutmeg

Mix first 7 ingredients together in a large bowl. Sift remaining ingredients together over the mixture and mix well. Pour into a greased and floured 9"x13" pan. Bake at 350° for 50-60 minutes. Cool in the pan or serve while still warm.

Serves 20

Blender Banana Tea Bread

2 eggs
½ c. soft butter or shortening
2 small ripe bananas, sliced
¾ c. sugar
1¾ c. sifted flour
¾ tsp. baking soda
1¼ tsp. cream of tartar
½ tsp. salt

Put first 4 ingredients into blender container. Cover and blend on high speed 20 seconds. Sift dry ingredients together into a mixing bowl. Pour egg mixture over and stir until just moistened. Turn into a greased loaf pan and bake in a preheated 350° oven for about 45 minutes.

Yields 15-20 slices

White Sulphur Springs
RANCH
BED AND BREAKFAST

P.O. Box 136 (Hwy. 89) • Clio, California 96106
(916) 836-2387

Enjoy this early colonial built in 1852, with its large warm spring-fed swimming pool and spacious grounds. Close to golf courses, overlooking Mohawk and Plumas Eureka State Park. An hour's drive from Reno, Truckee or Lake Tahoe.

Butter Brittle

2 packets of soda crackers
1 c. brown sugar
1 c. butter
2 c. chocolate chips
1 c. chopped nuts

Crush crackers fine. Put into 15"×10" greased jelly roll pan. Combine sugar and butter. Boil for three minutes. Pour evenly over crushed crackers. Place into 400 degree oven for five minutes. Remove and spread chips over top immediately. Let melt a couple of minutes. Spread evenly with a spoon. Sprinkle with chipped nuts. Let cool and cut into squares. Store in a covered container. Can be frozen.

Yield 2-3 dozen

Chocolate Cheesecake Muffins

3 oz. pkg. (or more) cream cheese
2 tbsp. granulated sugar
1 c. flour
½ c. sugar
3 tbsp. unsweetened cocoa
2 tsp. baking powder
½ tsp. salt
1 beaten egg
¾ c. milk
⅓ c. oil

In small bowl blend cream cheese and granulated sugar until fluffy. Set aside. (Can also add ½ cup chopped walnuts if desired.) In large bowl stir flour, sugar, cocoa, baking powder and salt. Make well in center of dry ingredients. Combine egg, milk and oil. Add all at once to dry ingredients, stirring until moistened. (Batter should be lumpy.) Spoon about 1 tbsp. chocolate batter into each muffin cup. Drop 1 tsp. cream cheese on top and then more chocolate batter. Bake at 375° for 20 minutes. Dust with powdered sugar if desired.

Yields 1 dozen

Orange Tea Muffins

1½ c. flour
½ c. sugar
2 tsp. baking powder
½ tsp. salt
½ c. butter or margarine (butter is better)
½ c. fresh orange juice
2 eggs
Grated rind of one orange

Combine flour, sugar, baking powder and salt. Blend well. Set aside. Melt butter. Take off heat and stir orange juice, egg and orange rind, beating well. Stir liquid into dry mix and blend until just moistened. Spoon into muffin cups. Make up mixture of sugar and small amount of orange juice. Mix and place on top of batter. Bake at 375° 15-20 minutes or until done.

Yields 1 dozen

HUMBOLDT COUNTY INNS

Each of our Humboldt County inns is unique, reflecting the personality of its innkeepers. We strive to offer you the finest hospitality in warm and inviting settings. Awaiting you is a romantic retreat with an opportunity to meet other travelers and to acquaint yourself with our beautiful county.

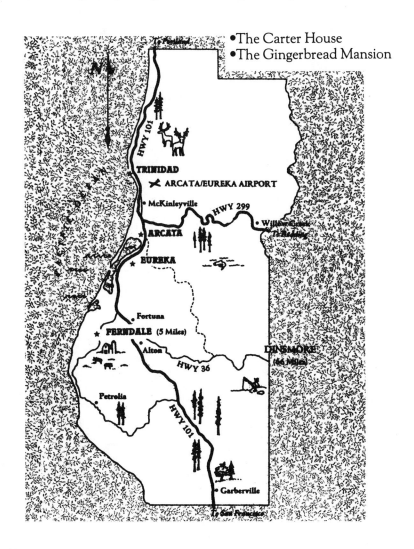

•The Carter House
•The Gingerbread Mansion

Carter House

1033 Third Street • Eureka, California 95501
(707) 445-1390

An enchanting Victorian mansion on a hillside at the door to "Old Town" with views of the Bay and the world-renowned Carson Mansion. Warm hospitality, irresistible food, and exquisite architecture make this inn a very special place to stay.

67

Pears Poached in Wine Sauce

8 pears
2 c. burgundy wine
2 tbsp. lemon juice
1 c. sugar
2 tsp. cinnamon
Zest of 1 lemon
1 tsp. vanilla extract
4 oz. whipping cream
16 mint leaves

Peel the pears, cut in half and core. Place the pears in a deep saucepan. In another saucepan bring the wine, lemon juice, sugar, cinnamon, lemon zest and vanilla to a boil. Pour the liquid over the pears and simmer slowly until the pears are tender, 10 to 20 minutes. Carefully remove the pear halves from the liquid. Place the pears on individual serving dishes. Boil the liquid down until it is reduced by half. Pour the wine sauce over the pears. Whip the whipping cream with an electric beater until soft peaks form. Place the whipped cream in a pastry bag and decorate the pear with the cream. Use the mint leaf to garnish the dish.

Serves 16

Raspberry Muffins

BATTER:

1½ c. all-purpose flour
½ c. granulated sugar
¼ c. packed dark brown sugar
2 tsp. baking powder
¼ tsp. salt
1 tbsp. cinnamon
1 egg, lightly beaten
½ c. (1 stick) unsalted butter
½ c. milk
1 c. fresh raspberries
1 tsp. grated lemon zest

STREUSEL TOPPING:

½ c. chopped pecans
½ c. packed dark brown sugar
¼ c. unbleached all-purpose flour
1 tsp. grated lemon zest
2 tbsp. unsalted butter, melted

Preheat oven to 350°F. Grease 12 muffin tins. Sift the flour, granulated sugar, brown sugar, baking powder, salt, and cinnamon together into a mixing bowl and make a well in the center. Place the egg, melted butter, and milk in the well. Stir until the ingredients are just combined. Quickly add the raspberries and lemon zest. Fill each muffin cup ⅔ full.

To make the streusel topping, combine the pecans, brown sugar, flour, cinnamon and lemon zest in a small bowl. Pour in the melted butter and stir to combine. Sprinkle this mixture over the top of each muffin. Bake until nicely browned, 20 to 25 minutes.

Serves 12

Eggs Jerusalem in an Orange Champagne Sauce

2 large artichokes
1 lemon, halved
2 small carrots
Salt and pepper to taste
2 eggs
1 tsp. of chives

Bring a large pot of water to a boil. Cut the stems off the artichokes and rub with the halved lemon. Cut off the top leaves just above the choke and discard them. Rub the tops of the artichoke with lemon. Squeeze the remaining lemon juice into the boiling water and boil for about 25 minutes or until the bottoms can be easily pierced with a knife. Cook the carrots in lightly salted boiling water until tender. Cut the carrots and puree in a food processor. Reserve the carrot puree.

Once the artichokes have cooked, cool them under running water. Remove the remaining leaves and chokes and trim the hearts to a nice round shape. Push the bottom of the artichoke hearts flat. Place the hearts on a plate in a warm oven. Spoon carrot puree on artichoke hearts. Bring another pan of water to a boil. Remove the pan of water from the heat and poach two eggs for 3 to 4 minutes in the water. Remove from water and place on artichoke hearts. Orange Champagne Sauce recipe follows.

Orange Champagne Sauce

½ c. freshly squeezed orange juice
½ c. champagne
¼ pound (1 stick) unsalted butter

In a heavy saucepan, combine orange juice and champagne and reduce liquid until it becomes a glaze (reduce by three-fourths). Remove pan from heat and whisk in 2 tbsp. of butter. Return to the heat and whisk in the remaining butter. When all the butter is incorporated, the sauce will have the consistency of Hollandaise.

To assemble, place each artichoke bottom on a warm plate with carrot puree and egg on top. Spoon the champagne sauce over the egg and artichoke and garnish with chives.

Morning Glory Muffins

2 c. flour
1 c. sugar
2 tsp baking soda
2 tsp cinnamon
1 apple, peeled, cored & grated
½ c. raisins
½ c. shredded coconut
½ c. pecans, chopped
1 c. grated carrot
3 eggs
½ c. vegetable oil
½ c. unsalted butter, melted
2 tsp vanilla extract

Sift flour, sugar, baking soda and cinnamon into a large mixing bowl. Add the grated apple, raisins, coconut, chopped pecans and grated carrots. Mix together thoroughly, until mixture resembles a coarse meal.

In a separate bowl, beat the eggs slightly. Add the vegetable oil, melted butter, and vanilla extract. Pour the wet ingredients into the dry and quickly combine. Spoon the batter into 24 well-greased muffin tins. Bake at 350° for 20-25 minutes, until golden brown.

Serves 24

The Gingerbread Mansion

400 Berding Street • Ferndale, California 95536
(707) 786-4000

Irresistible Victorian elegance in the fairytale village of Ferndale! Five large, romantic guestrooms in one of Northern California's most-photographed homes. Afternoon tea by the parlor fire, bicycles, bedside chocolates and beautiful gardens. One quiet block from the village.

73

Very Lemony Lemon Bread

½ c. shortening
1 c. sugar
2 eggs, slightly beaten
1¼ c. sifted flour (before measuring)
1 tsp. baking powder
½ tsp. salt
½ c. milk
½ c. finely chopped nuts
Grated peel of 1 lemon

TOPPING:
¼ c. sugar
Juice of 1 lemon

Cream shortening with sugar. Mix in eggs. Sift flour again with baking powder and salt. Alternately add flour mixture and the milk to shortening mixture, stirring constantly. Mix in the nuts and lemon peel. Bake in a greased 5"x9" loaf pan for about 50 minutes at 350°.

Poke holes in the top of the loaf with a fork. Combine the ¼ cup sugar with the lemon juice and pour over the top of the loaf while it is still hot.

Yields one 5x9" loaf

Pumpkin Gingerbread

SIFT TOGETHER:
3½ c. all-purpose flour
2 tsp. soda
1½ tsp. salt
½ tsp. baking powder
2 tsp. ginger
1 tsp. cinnamon
1 tsp. nutmeg
1 tsp. cloves
1 tsp. allspice

CREAM TOGETHER:
3 c. sugar
1 c. salad oil
4 eggs

⅔ c. water
1 1-lb. can of pumpkin

Add sifted ingredients and ⅔ cup water alternately to creamed mixture. Beat in one 1-lb. can of pumpkin. Pour into 2 greased 5"x9" loaf pans. Bake at 350° for 1 hour or until done.

Yields two 5"x9" loaves

Apple Loaf Cake

2 c. sugar
½ c. corn (or salad) oil
2 eggs
2 c. flour
2 tsp. cinnamon
2 tsp. baking soda
½ tsp. salt
1 tsp. vanilla
4 c. diced (and peeled) apples
1 c. nuts
½ c. raisins

Mix together sugar, oil, eggs. Add flour, cinnamon, baking soda, salt and vanilla. Mix well. Add diced apples and nuts and raisins Bake in 5"x9" loaf pan at 350° for 45 minutes or until done.

Yields 1 loaf

MARIN COUNTY
INNS

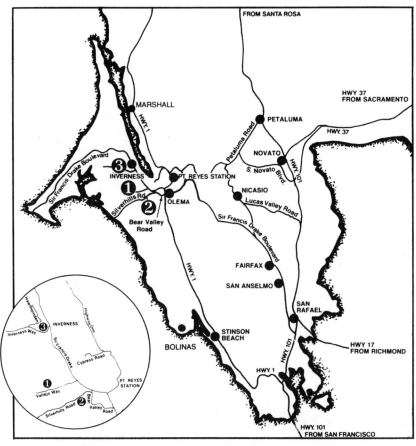

❶ Blackthorne Inn, PO Box 712, Inverness, CA 94937. At 266 Vallejo Avenue, off Sir Francis Drake Boulevard, in Inverness Park. (415) 663-8621

❷ Holly Tree Inn, PO Box 642, Point Reyes Station, CA 94956. Look for the inn sign on Bear Valley Road, 1.8 miles from park headquarters. (415) 663-1554

❸ Ten Inverness Way, PO Box 63, Inverness, CA 94937. Turn left on Inverness Way—look for the inn sign on Sir Francis Drake Boulevard. (415) 669-1648

BLACKTHORNE INN

P.O. Box 712, 266 Vallejo Ave. • Inverness, California 94937
(415) 663-8621

A "carpenter's fantasy" according to Sunset Magazine, this unique treehouse-like structure rises through fragrant bay trees to sunny decks on four levels. Five rooms. Includes breakfast and hot tub.

Blackthorne's Fudge Ribbon Cake

2 tbsp. butter
8 oz. pkg. cream cheese
2¼ c. sugar
1 tbsp. cornstarch
3 eggs
1⅓ c. milk plus 2 tbsp.
1½ tsp. vanilla extract
2 c. sifted flour
1 tsp. salt
1 tsp. baking powder
1 tsp. baking soda
½ c. butter (room temperature)
4 squares unsweetened chocolate

Cream butter with cream cheese, ¼ cup sugar and cornstarch. Add 1 egg, 2 tbsp. milk and ½ tsp. vanilla extract. Beat at high speed with mixer until smooth and creamy.

Grease and flour bottom of 13"x9" pan. Combine flour with remaining 2 cups sugar, salt, baking powder and soda in large mixing bowl. Add ½ cup butter and 1 cup milk. Blend well at low speed. Beat 1½ minutes at low speed. Add remaining ⅓ cup milk, 2 eggs, melted unsweetened chocolate, and vanilla extract; continue beating 1½ minutes at low speed. Spread half of batter in 13"x9" pan. Spoon cheese mixture over batter, spreading carefully to cover. Top with remaining batter; spread to cover. Bake at 350° for 50 to 60 minutes until cake springs back when touched lightly in center. Cool and frost. (Recipe follows.)

Serves 12 plus

Chocolate Frosting

¼ c. milk
¼ c. butter
6 oz. chocolate chips
1 tsp. vanilla
2½ c. sifted confectioner's sugar

Combine milk and butter in saucepan; bring to a boil. Remove from heat. Blend in chocolate chips. Stir in vanilla extract and confectioner's sugar. Beat until spreading consistency. If necessary, thin with a few drops of milk.

ᴴOLLY TREE INN

Box 642 • Point Reyes Station, California 94956
(415) 663-1554

Tucked away on a forest hillside, yet pleasantly close to town, bay, or beach. Cozy corner rooms. Rates include full country breakfast, and the run of a lovely living room with enormous fireplace.

83

Creamed Holly Tree Inn Duck-Eggs with Onion Toast

ONION TOAST:
1 small onion minced
¼ lb. plus 2 tbsp. butter
1 tbsp. Dijon mustard
¼ tsp. black pepper
16 slices of French bread, medium thick with crust trimmed
Paprika

SAUCE:
2 tbsp. butter
2 tbsp. flour
1 c. scalded milk
2 oz. cheese (Jarlsburg, cheddar, or fontina)
Parmesan cheese, grated
8 hard boiled duck eggs, sliced or extra jumbo chicken eggs
Paprika

ONION TOAST:
Melt butter in frying pan and saute onions until they begin to brown. Add Dijon mustard, pepper and more butter. Brush on both sides of bread, dust with paprika. Bake on a cookie sheet, 10 minutes each side or until toasted to desired dryness. Do ahead and warm in oven wrapped in tinfoil for 5 minutes.

SAUCE:
Melt butter and add flour, cook 2 minutes and whisk in the milk, stirring until it thickens. Grate cheese, add to sauce and stir. Taste sauce and correct with salt or pepper. Butter ramekins and dust with grated parmesan cheese. Arrange sliced egg in a crescent shape in ramekin and spoon sauce over the top. Sprinkle lightly with grated parmesan and paprika. Broil till cheese bubbles. Serve with onion toast.

Makes 8 servings

Poppy Seed Bread

¼ c. butter or margarine
1 c. sugar
2 eggs
1 tsp. grated orange peel
2 c. all-purpose flour, unsifted
2½ tsp. baking powder
½ tsp. salt
¼ tsp. ground nutmeg
1 c. milk
⅓ c. poppy seed
½ c. chopped nuts
½ c. golden raisins (optional)
Tangy apricot spread (recipe follows)

Beat together butter and sugar until smoothly blended; add eggs, one at a time, beating well after each addition. Mix in orange peel. In a separate bowl, stir together flour, baking powder, salt, and nutmeg until thoroughly blended. Add flour mixture alternately with milk to creamed mixture until well blended, then stir in poppy seed, nuts and raisins (if used). Turn batter into a well-greased and flour-dusted 9"x5" loaf pan.

Bake in a 350° oven for 1 hour and 10 minutes or until bread begins to pull away from sides of pan and a wooden skewer inserted in center comes out clean. Cool completely.

Yield 1 loaf

Tangy Apricot Spread

½ c. soft butter or margarine
¼ c. apricot jam
1 tsp. grated lemon peel
1 tbsp. lemon juice

Beat together butter or margarine, apricot jam, grated lemon peel, and lemon juice.

Minted Melon Balls

⅓ c. sugar
½ c. water
1½ tbsp. coarsely chopped fresh mint or 2 tsp. dry mint
2 tbsp. orange juice
1 tbsp. lemon juice
8 c. assorted melon balls or bite size pieces
Mint sprigs

In a small pan over high heat, combine sugar and water; bring to a boil, stirring until sugar is dissolved; then boil for five minutes. Remove from heat and pour over mint; cover and chill for 1 hour. Strain syrup through a wire strainer and discard mint. Stir in orange juice and lemon juice; cover and chill. Pour chilled syrup over melon balls and garnish with mint sprigs.

Serves 6-8

TEN INVERNESS WAY
BED AND BREAKFAST

P.O. Box 63 • Inverness, California 94937
(415) 669-1648

Comfortable 1904 inn in charming coastal village. Country garden, hearty breakfasts, handmade quilts, and all the activities of the Point Reyes National Seashore. "One of the niftiest inns in Northern California . . . snug as a Christmas stocking, as cheery as a roaring fire." (Jerry Hulse, L.A. Times)

87

Banana (or Blackberry) Buttermilk Buckwheat Pancakes

⅓ c. white flour
⅓ c. buckwheat flour
⅓ c. whole wheat flour
1 tbsp. sugar
½ tsp. salt
½ tsp. soda
2 tsp. baking powder
1 beaten egg
2 tbsp. oil
1 c. buttermilk
1 ripe mashed banana
  Or 1 c. blackberries, whole, washed

Combine dry ingredients. In a separate bowl combine egg, oil and buttermilk and add to dry ingredients. Stir just until mixed. Drop by ⅓ cupfuls on 350° griddle.

Serves 2 or 3

Strata

14-16 slices dry bread
1 chopped onion
6 tbsp. melted butter
½ lb. smoked cheese
½ lb. cheddar cheese
14 eggs
3 c. milk
⅓ tsp. red pepper
¼ tsp. pepper
1 tbsp. Dijon mustard
½ c. white wine

Grease a 9"x13" pan well. Cut or break bread into fourths. Toss with chopped onion and put into pan. Spread melted butter over bread. Grate cheeses and sprinkle over bread. Beat together eggs and other ingredients until foamy. Pour over bread. Refrigerate up to 24 hours. Bakes at 325° for 1½ hours, covered with foil. Uncover and bake 10 minutes more. Let stand 15 minutes before cutting.

Serves 8-10

Fruit-Topped Kuchen

½ c. margarine
½ c. honey
1½ c. whole wheat flour
2 eggs
¾ tsp. baking powder
⅓ c. milk
1 tsp. vanilla
Fresh fruit

In a saucepan melt margarine. Add honey and mix well. Cool.
Add remaining ingredients, except fresh fruit. Mix well and pour
into a 9"x13" pan which has been greased and floured. Cover
with fresh fruit halves, skin side up. Or sprinkle generously with
fresh blackberries. Bake at 350° for 45 minutes or until golden
brown on top and a toothpick test is passed.

Serves 6 generously

MENDOCINO COAST INNS

- •Elk Cove Inn
- •The Grey Whale Inn
- •Joshua Grindle Inn
- •Toll House Inn
- •Whale Watch Inn by the Sea

ELK COVE INN

Hwy. One (P.O. Box 367) • Elk, California 95432
(707) 877-3321

1883 Victorian with spectacular ocean views. Gourmet meals are French/German specialties. Beds have the subtle luxury of sun-dried linens. Antiques, fireplaces, libraries, private beach. Relaxed-romantic atmosphere in a rural village.

93

Orange Souffle Omelette

2 tbsp. butter
5 eggs, separated
Dash of cream of tartar
1 tbsp. sugar
2 tbsp. flour
½ tsp. baking powder
½ tsp. vanilla flavoring
½ tsp. each dried orange peel and lemon peel
½ c. freshly squeezed and strained orange juice
1 c. sour cream
1 c. whole berry cranberry sauce
Orange slices

Melt butter in skillet. Beat egg whites with cream of tartar and sugar until *barely* stiff. Blend the flour, baking powder, and peel in a bowl. Stir in orange juice, egg yolks and vanilla flavoring and beat until frothy. Gently fold into beaten egg whites. Pour and spread this mixture into the skillet. Cook tightly covered (300°) for about 8 minutes or until golden brown on bottom and just firm. Cut into quarters. Turn each quarter over carefully in place and cook another 5 minutes.

Mix sour cream and cranberry sauce together and serve on the side of the omelette. Garnish with orange slices.

Serves 2

Date-White Raisin Muffins

3 c. flour
3 tsp. baking powder
1 tsp. baking soda
½ c. date sugar (available in specialty stores)
2 large eggs
1½ c. buttermilk
½ tsp. vanilla flavoring
½ c. oil
⅔ c. white raisins
3 tbsp. turbinado or raw sugar

Sift together flour, baking powder, baking soda and date sugar. In separate bowl beat eggs, buttermilk and vanilla flavoring. Add to flour mixture. Add oil. Quickly stir together with spoon to blend (do not overblend). Add white raisins. Spoon into 12 buttered muffin tins. Sprinkle with turbinado sugar. Bake 20 minutes at 350°.

Yields 12 muffins

"Eierkuchen"

(German Egg Cakes)

⅔ c. flour
¾ tsp. baking powder
¼ tsp. baking soda
½ c. buttermilk
10 large eggs, separated
1 tsp. vanilla flavoring
¼ tsp. cream of tartar
1 tbsp. sugar
Unsalted butter

TOPPINGS:

1 c. sweetened whipped cream
1 tbsp. sour cream blended together with whipped cream
Blackberries, strawberries or any hot, thickened berry sauce

In a bowl sift together flour, baking powder and baking soda. Add buttermilk, egg yolks and vanilla flavoring. Beat. In a large bowl beat egg whites until stiff with cream of tartar and sugar. Gently fold flour/egg yolk mixture into beaten egg whites. Preheat griddle or frying pan to 325°. Brush with butter. For each egg cake, spoon about ½ cup batter onto griddle. Turn egg cakes over with a spatula when bottom becomes golden brown, continue cooking until golden on second side and edges feel dry, 7-8 minutes total. Serve at once. Whipped cream/sour cream mixture and berries or hot berry sauce for topping.

Serves 4

615 North Main Street • Fort Bragg, California 95437
(707) 964-0640 — 1-800-FTBRAGG

In the beautifully landscaped 1915 Redwood Coast Hospital building,
John and Colette Bailey provide a welcoming atmosphere of light,
spacious rooms filled with their own collections of books, paintings, and
post-war furnishings and the fragrances of Colette's prize-winning cakes
and breads.

Spiced Tomato Juice

1 46 oz. can tomato juice
2 tbsp. dillweed
1 tsp. Spike seasoning
¼ tsp. garlic powder
1 tsp. Worcestershire sauce
1 tsp. lemon juice

Mix together the night before so that flavors will blend well.

Fresh Apple Cake

2 c. walnuts
½ c. plus 2 tbsp. sugar
2 tbsp. cinnamon
6 apples, peeled and thinly sliced

6 c. flour
2 tbsp. plus 2 tsp. baking powder

4 c. sugar
2 c. corn oil
8 eggs
1 tbsp. plus 1 tsp. vanilla
½ c. orange juice

Place walnuts in a food processor and finely chop. Add next 3 ingredients and mix together. Sift flour and baking powder together. Cream next 5 ingredients.

Combine dry ingredients with creamed ingredients. Grease and flour two 12-inch tube pans. Spoon ½ batter into pans, then ½ apple-nut mixture; repeat ending with apple mixture on top. Bake at 350°. Check cake after 1 hour 40 minutes for doneness. Cool for 15 minutes before removing from pan.

Serves approximately 24

Cranberry Coffee Cake

1½ c. softened margarine
3 c. sugar
6 eggs
1 tbsp. almond extract

6 c. flour
1 tbsp. baking powder
1 tbsp. baking soda
1½ tsp. salt

3 c. sour cream
2 — 16 oz. cans whole cranberry sauce
1 c. chopped walnuts

Cream margarine and sugar until light and fluffy. Add eggs, one at a time, beat thoroughly after each addition. Beat in almond extract. Sift dry ingredients together. Add dry ingredients to creamed mixture alternately with sour cream, beating well after each addition. Grease and flour two 12-inch tube pans. Preheat oven to 350°.

Spoon ⅓ batter into pans. Crumble ⅓ cranberry sauce over batter. Repeat layers twice, ending with sauce. Sprinkle nuts over top. Bake for 1 hour and 15 minutes. Test for doneness. Let cool 5 minutes before removing from pans. Drizzle glaze on top. (Recipe follows.)

Glaze

1½ c. powdered sugar
1 tsp. almond extract
2 tbsp. warm water

Mix glaze ingredients together.

Basic Crustless Quiche

1 qt. cottage cheese
1 c. finely grated Romano cheese
8 eggs
¼ tsp. grated nutmeg
¼ tsp. coarsely ground black pepper
4 tbsp. butter
1 c. minced onions
3 c. thoroughly drained chopped spinach or
    2 c. finely minced broccoli
1 c. sliced mushrooms
¾ c. milk
Paprika or sliced tomatoes
Cilantro or parsley

Put first 5 ingredients in food processor and process until thoroughly mixed and cottage cheese is smooth. Grease baking pan. In skillet, saute butter and minced onion. Cook until soft over moderate heat, stirring well. Add spinach or broccoli and mushrooms. Remove skillet from heat and add milk. Let mixture cool 5 minutes, then combine with cheese-egg mixture. Pour into greased 9"x13" baking dish. Sprinkle lightly with paprika or tomatoes arranged over top of quiche mixture. Bake at 375° for 35 minutes. Garnish with cilantro or curly parsley. Let quiche cool for about 10 minutes before cutting into portions.

Serves 12-15

JOSHUA GRINDLE INN

44800 Little Lake, P.O. Box 647 • Mendocino, California 95460
(707) 937-4143

An impressive New England style Victorian overlooking Mendocino and the ocean. Early American antiques furnish each comfortable room. Fireplaces, views, private baths. Accommodations are also available in our cottage and watertower.

103

Applesauce Muffins

4½ c. flour
1¼ c. sugar
4½ tsp. baking powder
2¼ tsp. salt
1¼ tsp. soda
1 tsp. allspice
1 jar (25 oz.) applesauce or 2 c. homemade applesauce
½ c. white raisins
3 eggs
¾ c. milk
¾ c. oil

Combine flour, sugar, baking powder, salt, soda and allspice in a large bowl. In another bowl combine applesauce, raisins, eggs, milk and oil. Stir. (Let wet ingredients sit covered overnight in the refrigerator.) Add wet ingredients to dry and mix until dry ingredients are moistened. Fill muffin cups, sprayed with Pam, ⅔ full. Bake at 375° for 15 minutes or until done.

Yields 34-36 Muffins

Strawberry Muffins

4½ c. flour
1¼ c. sugar
2¼ tbsp. baking powder
1⅔ tsp. salt
1¼ tsp. baking soda
1 pint chopped strawberries
3 eggs, slightly beaten
1 tsp. almond extract
2¼ c. buttermilk
1 stick (¼ lb.) margarine, melted
¼ c. sugar, 2 tbsp. cinnamon   topping

Combine flour, sugar, baking powder, salt and baking soda. Add chopped strawberries. Mix. Add eggs, almond extract, buttermilk and margarine. Mix until dry ingredients are moistened. Fill greased muffin cups ⅔ full. (Spray muffin tins with Pam.) Top with cinnamon/sugar mixture. Bake at 375° for 15 minutes or until done.

Yields 36 Muffins

Crustless Quiche

½ c. butter
12 eggs
½ c. flour (Wondra)
1 tsp. baking powder
2 tbsp. butter
1 8 oz. can green chiles, chopped
1 pint cottage cheese
1 lb. jack cheese (grated)

Grease 13"x9"x2" pan. (Spray pan with Pam.) Melt butter. Beat eggs lightly. Add flour and baking powder, then blend. Add butter, chiles, cottage cheese and jack cheese. Mix until just blended. Pour into pan. Bake at 400° for 15 minutes, then 350° for 35-40 minutes. Check to make sure it is baked clear through.

Serves 10-12

Anytime Muffins

2 c. rolled oats
2 c. boiling water
4 eggs, beaten
2 c. sugar
1 c. oil
1 qt. buttermilk
3 c. whole wheat flour
2 c. all-purpose flour
5 tsp. baking soda
1 tsp. salt
4 c. All Bran cereal

Combine oats and boiling water; let cool. Mix together eggs, oats, sugar, oil, and buttermilk; stir in sifted dry ingredients with All Bran just until moistened. Store in covered containers in refrigerator up to 6 weeks. Bake in well greased muffin tins. Raisins, nuts, or chopped dates may be added to batter before baking at 375° degrees, 15 to 20 minutes.

Yields 5-6 dozen Muffins

The Toll House

15301 Hwy. 253, P.O. Box 268 • Boonville, California 95415
(707) 895-3630

The Toll House Inn lies secluded in Bell Valley in the heart of Mendocino Wine Country. The serenity of the inn carries guests back to a time when life was less hurried.

Meda's Coffee Cake

2 c. all-purpose flour
1 tsp. nutmeg
1 tsp. cinnamon
1 tsp. baking powder
1 tsp. soda
1 tsp. salt
1 c. brown sugar
¾ c. salad oil
1 egg, beaten
1 c. buttermilk

Sift dry ingredients. Add brown sugar and oil. Blend, saving ¼ cup for topping. Then add slightly beaten egg and buttermilk. Bake in greased 8" square pan sprinkled with topping for 35 minutes at 325°.

Serves 8

INN BY THE SEA

35100 Hwy. One • Gualala, California 95445
(707) 884-3667

Oceanside retreat—eighteen luxurious, contemporary accommodations in five buildings overlooking Anchor Bay. Outstanding ocean views, beach access, private decks. Most have whirlpool tubs in room and fireplaces, five have kitchens. Adults only, no pets, smoking permitted on decks only. Visa, MasterCard, American Express welcome.

Melted Brie with Almonds

1 wedge of brie cheese
2-3 tbsp. melted butter
¼ c. toasted, sliced almonds or chopped walnuts

Score a wedge of brie cheese along surface. Pour melted butter over brie. Sprinkle with toasted, sliced almonds or chopped nuts. Heat on high in microwave, rotating at 7 second intervals until partially melted. Serve with crackers as an appetizer.

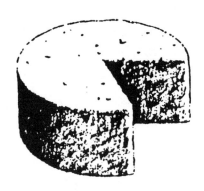

Frittata

10 eggs
½ c. flour
1 tsp. baking powder
½ tsp. salt
1 pint small curd cottage cheese

1 lb. shredded jack cheese
½ c. melted butter
8 oz. diced green chiles

Place eggs in mixer and beat. Add flour, baking powder, salt and cottage cheese. Stir in cheese, butter and green chiles. Pour into greased 9"x13" pan. Bake at 350° for 35 minutes.

Serves 12-15

Mushroom Crust Quiche

5 tbsp. butter
½ lb. mushrooms, chopped
½ c. finely crushed saltine crackers
¾ c. chopped green onions
2 c. (8 oz.) shredded jack or Swiss cheese
1 c. cottage cheese
3 eggs
¼ tsp. each cayenne and paprika

In a frying pan over medium heat, melt 3 tbsp. butter, add mushroom and cook until limp. Stir in crushed saltines, then turn mixture evenly over bottom and sides of pan. In the same frying pan over medium heat, melt 2 tbsp. butter, add onion and cook until limp. Spread onions over mushroom crust; sprinkle evenly with shredded cheese. In a blender, whirl cottage cheese, eggs and cayenne until smooth. Pour into crust and sprinkle with paprika. Bake in 350° oven for 20-25 minutes or until knife inserted off center comes out clean. Let stand 10-15 minutes before cutting. Freezes well. Rewarm 15 minutes in 325° oven.

Serves 4-6

NAPA VALLEY INNS

Napa Valley is beautiful all year. . .In winter, the hills are a thousand shades of green. In spring, the hills abound with wildflowers. Black, sknarled grapevines contrast sharply with yellow mustard. In summer, the green vineyards beautifully compliment the golden hills surrounding our valley. In fall, the grape harvest ("crush") is in full swing as the grape leaves turn colors from amber through red. Any season in the Napa Valley is a special time. The only thing missing is you!

The Valley is synonymous with fine wines and great restaurants. Hot air balloons, gliders, spas, and wineries invite you to visit. The best way to sample all we have to offer is to spend a few days in our valley.

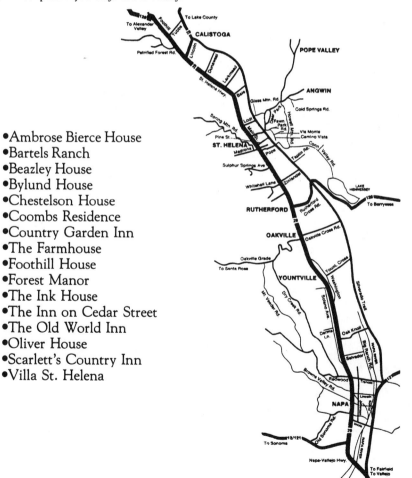

- Ambrose Bierce House
- Bartels Ranch
- Beazley House
- Bylund House
- Chestelson House
- Coombs Residence
- Country Garden Inn
- The Farmhouse
- Foothill House
- Forest Manor
- The Ink House
- The Inn on Cedar Street
- The Old World Inn
- Oliver House
- Scarlett's Country Inn
- Villa St. Helena

115

Ambrose Bierce House

1515 Main Street • St. Helena, California 94574
(707) 963-3003

Combine the history of four of Napa's most intriguing characters with the pampering of one of the wine country's most enchanting bed and breakfast inns. Brass beds, clawfoot tubs, armoires and lovely gardens create an atmosphere of relaxation and charm.

Compote of Dried Fruit in Apple Juice

½-⅔ c. dried apricots (unsulphured)
½-⅔ c. dried apples
½-⅔ c. dried prunes
½ c. white raisins (muscats)
¼ c. raisins
2 c. apple juice
1 inch cinnamon stick
Thinly pared rind of 1 lemon

Put the fruit into a bowl and cover it with the apple juice. Put in the cinnamon stick and lemon rind and leave the fruit to soak for 12 hours. Remove the lemon rind and cut it into thin strips. Put the fruit, cinnamon stick and lemon rind into a saucepan. Set on low heat and bring gently to a boil. Simmer for 15 minutes. Remove the cinnamon stick. Either serve the compote hot or let it cool completely and serve it topped with natural yogurt or sour cream.

Serves 4-6

Orange and Lemon Whip

8 medium-sized oranges
Juice of ½ lemon
4 tbsp. clear honey
2½ c. plain yogurt
4 tbsp. chopped nuts (walnuts, filberts, almonds or hazelnuts)

Thinly pare 3 strips of the rind of one of the oranges and finely chop and reserve it. Cut all the peel and white fibre or pith from this and all the remaining oranges. Finely chop the flesh, removing all the seeds and put it into a blender with the lemon juice, honey and yogurt. Work them together so you have a smooth, thick puree. Pour the mixture into individual serving glasses and sprinkle each one with chopped nuts and the reserved orange rind.

Serves 4-6

1200 Conn Valley Road • St. Helena, California 94574
(707) 963-4001

Secluded romantic country estate offers the perfect wine country weekend. Three elegantly decorated guestrooms with antiques, private baths, recreation room with fireplace, pool table, pool/jacuzzi. Continental breakfast, wines and warm hospitality.

Mom's Million Dollar Nut Bars

1½ c. sugar
2 eggs
1 c. warm water
1 tsp. vanilla
2 c. flour
2 tsp. baking powder
½ tsp. salt

Powdered Sugar Icing:
   1½ c. powdered sugar
   1 cube butter
   1 tsp. vanilla
   1 c. boiling water

Ground salted peanuts

Beat sugar and eggs 3 minutes. Add warm water and vanilla. Set aside. Sift 3 times flour, baking powder and salt. Add to above sugar/egg mixture. Pour in regular cake pan 13"x9" at 350°. Bake 35 minutes. Mix together icing ingredients. Cool cake, then cut in squares approximately 1½" x 3". Dip in thin powdered sugar icing and roll in ground salted peanuts. Cool and serve. Can be frozen and served later.

Approx. 27 Bars

Jami's Potatoes Magnifique!

10 sliced boiled potatoes
2 pints sour cream
4 — 8 oz. pkgs. cream cheese
Pimento
1 large onion
Curry powder
Ground red pepper
Thyme
Basil
Parsley
1½ lb. shredded sharp cheddar cheese
Paprika

In a 5 quart casserole, layer the first 5 ingredients. Lightly sprinkle between layers the next 5 ingredients. Cover with shredded sharp cheddar cheese. Sprinkle paprika on top of entire casserole. Heat in oven at 350° for 20 minutes or until bubbly and cheese has melted.

Serves 20

Beazley
House

A 1902 landmark mansion and carriage house in a lovely Victorian neighborhood in central Napa. It has 8 rooms, 5 with private baths and fireplaces, some with private spas. Visa/MasterCard.

125

Beazley House Buttermilk Blueberry Muffins

2 c. unbleached flour
⅓ c. sugar
2 tsp. baking powder
½ tsp. baking soda
1 scant c. fresh or frozen blueberries
1 c. buttermilk
⅓ c. oil
1 egg
Sugar

Preheat oven to 400°. Mix all dry ingredients and blueberries in one large mixing bowl. In separate container, mix wet ingredients thoroughly. Pour wet ingredients into dry, mix quickly with a large fork JUST UNTIL FLOUR DISAPPEARS. DO NOT OVERMIX. Batter should be LUMPY. Spoon into muffin tin sprayed with vegetable spray. Spinkle muffins with ½ tsp. sugar each, then bake for 20 to 25 minutes.

Serves 12

Beazley House Banana Nut Muffins

2 c. sugar
1 c. oil
4 eggs
2 c. VERY ripe bananas (pureed)
2 tsp. vanilla
4 c. unbleached flour
2 tsp. soda
4 tsp. baking powder
1 c. buttermilk
1½ c. chopped almonds

Mix sugar, oil and eggs until fluffy. Mix in bananas and vanilla. Add half the flour, the soda and baking powder. Mix until smooth. Mix in buttermilk. Add the remainder of the flour and beat until smooth. Add nuts. Spoon into 3 muffin tins (12 muffins each tin), which have been sprayed with Pam vegetable spray. Place in oven which has been preheated to 350°. Bake 25 minutes or until golden.

Serves 18 (makes 3 dozen)

BYLUND HOUSE

---❧---

2000 Howell Mt. Road • St. Helena, California 94574
(707) 963-9073

---❧---

Privacy in a romantic setting, with all the amenities to make your stay a memorable one, can be found at Bylund House in St. Helena. "Modern architecture in the tradition of a Northern Italian Villa" is how owners/hosts Bill and Diane Bylund describe their bed and breakfast inn, tucked away in a secluded valley area with all the activities just a short distance away.

Roquefort Rounds

1 tsp. garlic juice
3 oz. roquefort
½ c. mayonnaise
½ c. sour cream
¼ c. chopped chives
1 French Baguette

Mix first five ingredients well. Slice French bread into thin rounds. Spread mixture on each slice and place under broiler until golden brown. Serve piping hot.

Serves 6

Chesterton House

1417 Kearney Street • St. Helena, California 94574
(707) 963-2238

Victorian in the heart of the wine country. Residential neighborhood with a short walk to restaurants and shops. Queen beds, wraparound porch, gourmet breakfast and complimentary wine. Light, friendly atmosphere. Jackie Sweet, innkeeper.

131

South of the Border Eggs

12 hard boiled eggs
2 tbsp. Dijon mustard
3 tbsp. sour cream
Salt and pepper
1 small onion chopped
3 tbsp. oil or butter
1 4 oz. can Ortega chilles
1 can Cream of Mushroom soup — 10¾ oz.
1 c. sour cream
1 c. cheddar cheese, shredded

Cut hard boiled eggs in half and mash yolk with mustard and sour cream, adding extra sour cream if necessary to make a smooth filling for whites. Add salt and pepper to taste and stuff white halves. Place in 14 inch shallow baking dish. Saute onion in oil or butter, add chiles and stir in Cream of Mushroom soup and sour cream. Pour this mixture over stuffed eggs. Sprinkle with shredded cheddar cheese. Bake at 325° for 20-25 minutes. Garnish with parsley, cherry tomatoes or tortilla chips.

Serves 8

Wild Blackberry Coffee Cake

2 c. flour
1 c. sugar
2 tsp. baking powder
1 tsp. salt
1½ tsp. grated orange peel
½ c. (1 stick) margarine
2 eggs
1 c. milk
1 tsp. vanilla
3 c. blackberries (any kind of berries may be substituted for
    blackberries)

BROWN SUGAR TOPPING:
½ c. firmly packed brown sugar
¼ c. flour
1 tsp. cinnamon
2 tbsp. firm margarine

Measure flour, sugar, baking powder, salt and orange peel into food processor with chopping blade in place. Add margarine cut into four pieces and process with pulse, on and off until texture of cornmeal. Turn into bowl and add lightly beaten eggs mixed with milk and vanilla; stir until dry ingredients are moist. Pour into well greased tube pan. Sprinkle berries on top. Scatter berries with brown sugar topping which has been processed in the same manner as coffee cake mixture. Bake at 350° for 1 hour or until wooden toothpick comes out clean when inserted in the center.

Serves 8-10

---

720 Seminary Street • Napa, California 94559
(707) 257-0789

A lovely old two-story house built in 1852, this inn on the park has been completely restored and beautifully furnished in both old European and American antiques. Down comforters and pillows, luxurious personal terry robes and bath sheets add to the inn's charm and comfort.

Caramel Cheesecake

CRUST:
1 c. graham cracker crumbs
¼ c. finely chopped almonds
¼ c. sugar
6 tbsp. melted butter
½ tsp. cinnamon

FILLING:
32 oz. cream cheese
2 c. dark brown sugar (must be *dark* brown sugar)
4 eggs
1 tbsp. vanilla
½ tsp. salt
1 c. finely chopped toasted almonds

TOPPING:
2 c. sour cream
5 tbsp. sugar
½ tsp. vanilla
½ tsp. cinnamon
¼ c. sliced, toasted almonds

Combine graham cracker crumbs, chopped almonds, sugar, melted butter and cinnamon in bowl. Pat the mixture on the bottom and sides of a 9½ inch spring-form pan. Chill. Combine in a processor the cream cheese and dark brown sugar. Process until smooth, add eggs, one at a time and process until combined. Add vanilla, salt and toasted almonds. Process until just combined. Pour into prepared spring-form pan and bake for 1 hour and 15 minutes in 350° oven.

Combine sour cream, sugar, vanilla and cinnamon. Spread on slightly cooled cheesecake and bake 5 minutes longer. Remove from oven and sprinkle toasted sliced almonds around top edge of cheesecake.

Serves 10-12

Rhubarb Bread

1½ c. brown sugar
1 c. cooking oil
1 c. buttermilk
2 tsp. cinnamon
1 tsp. soda
1 tsp. salt
2½ c. unsifted flour
1 egg, beaten
1 tsp. vanilla
1½ c. chopped fresh rhubarb
1 c. chopped walnuts

TOPPING:
¼ c. sugar
1 tbsp. softened butter
¾ tsp. cinnamon

Cream brown sugar, oil and buttermilk together. Sift cinnamon, soda, salt and flour together. Fold into brown sugar buttermilk mixture. Add beaten egg and vanilla. Fold rhubarb and nuts into mixture. Pour into a 9"x5" oiled loaf pan and top with combined sugar, butter, cinnamon mixture. Bake 1 hour at 350°.

Serves 8-10

Oranges in Red Wine

1 c. red wine
¾ c. sugar
1 c. water
2 whole cloves
1 stick cinnamon
2 slices lemon
2 slices tangerines (in season)
6 large sliced navel oranges

Bring wine, sugar and water to a boil. Put cloves, cinnamon stick, lemon and tangerine slices in cheese cloth. Place cheese cloth in wine mixture; boil until liquid becomes syrup. Cool, then place sliced oranges in mixture and marinate overnight.

Serves 4

Country Garden Inn

1815 Silverado Trail • Napa, California 94558
(707) 255-1197

Situated on one and a half acres of mature woodland riverside property, the Country Garden Inn offers the Napa Valley visitor a secluded get away in the tradition of a fine European country inn.

139

Deviled Almonds

4 lbs. blanched almonds
½ c. salt
1 tbsp. cayenne pepper

Place almonds in large pan and just cover with water. Bring to a boil. Drain and allow to cool long enough to become semi-dry (about 5 minutes). Sprinkle with salt and mix until salt dissolves. Sprinkle on cayenne and mix well to ensure even coating. Spread on cookie sheet and bake in 200 degree oven for 14 to 16 hours. After 1 hour, mix nuts around to prevent sticking. Amount of cayenne can be varied according to taste and quality of cayenne.

English Afternoon Tea Scones

3 c. self-rising flour
4 oz. butter
½ tsp. salt
½ c. sugar
2 Eggs·
5 oz. milk

In a processor, mix flour and butter until crumbly. Add salt and sugar. Pulse 2 times. Add eggs. Pulse until mixed. Add milk. Pulse until dough forms. Roll on ½ inch thick. Cut with 2-inch cookie cutter. Bake in 400 degree oven 12 minutes or until golden brown. Serve with strawberry jam and whipped or clotted cream.

Rum Truffles

9 oz. chocolate
1½ tbsp. Half & Half
3 egg yolks
1½ oz. butter
3 tbsp. rum

Melt chocolate and Half & Half in pan over very low heat. Remove from heat. Add eggs, butter, and rum. Blend mixture until thick (in processor a good 5 minutes). Refrigerate. When cold, form into ¾" balls and toss in powdered chocolate—not cocoa. Given- one-half a chance, these freeze well!

Cup of Tea

The secret of making a really good cup of tea revolves around ensuring that the water is as near boiling as possible when it hits the tea leaves, and that the infusion takes place as rapidly as possible. To achieve this, you should:

1. Use a metal, preferably silver tea pot, as metal conducts heat better, and therefore the tea is infused hotter.
2. Heat the pot by swilling around with boil water. Pour out the water.
3. Immediately add loose tea leaves. If loose tea leaves are not available, use metal infuser. Tea bags are the worst choice as the tea in these is chopped fine and infusion in water is slow. Also the tea bag cover absorbs heat.
4. Boiling water at 212 degrees should be added. Never take the kettle to the tea pot. Always the tea pot to the kettle, because in the former, the water will go off the boil.

The ideal way is to have a kettle of boiling water kept hot by a small spirit stove on the table where the tea was being made.

If the water is below 209 degrees when it hits the tea leaves, don't expect a nice cup of tea. It is regretable, but don't expect a nice cup of tea in Denver, as at 7,000 feet the boiling point of water is 180 degrees; too low to make a good cup.

5. The tea should be allowed to draw for five minutes before serving. It can be kept warm under a tea cosy.
6. Milk, if taken, should be added to the tea cup before the tea. If milk is added to boiling tea, the milk is scalded and ruins the taste. Also, if good bone china is used, pouring boiling water on it will soon craze the glazing.
7. For those who prefer weak tea, do not just add less tea to the pot, pour out half a cup of tea and add hot water to taste.
8. Allow one teaspoonful of tea per person, plus one for the pot. This should not be varied. Allow to draw for longer for those who want strong tea.
9. After half the pot of tea has been drunk, you can add more hot water to the teapot; the resulting tea will still be drinkable.

As to the tea itself, any good quality tea can be used. Use Twinnings English Breakfast Ten in the morning and Earl Grey for afternoon tea.

THE FARMHOUSE
Country Bed and Breakfast

300 Taplin Road • St. Helena, California 94574
(707) 944-8430

Secluded 70-year-old Mission-style farmhouse surrounded by vineyards. Three guest rooms, each with private entrances (private/semi-private baths), veranda, courtyard, pool, fireplaces in common rooms, generous complimentary continental breakfast. Peaceful relaxation in a country home.

143

Beef Tartar

1 lb. top ground round or sirloin
½ c. green onions and tops—chopped fine
1 egg white
4 oz. chopped roasted walnuts
½ c. chopped fresh parsley
½ tsp. salt
1 tsp. pepper
*Beau monde to taste
1 tbsp. prepared mustard (optional)

Combine all ingredients. Form into loaf. Chill in refrigerator wrapped in Saran Wrap until ready to serve. Serve with buffet rye bread. An appetizer favorite!

---

*Available in gourmet stores and some supermarkets.

Serves 12

Cheese Souffle

3 tbsp. butter
1 tbsp. dry mustard
5 slices sour dough bread (cut into cubes)
½ lb. cheddar cheese, grated
6 slices uncooked bacon, cut into small pieces
3 eggs
2 c. milk
Salt and pepper

Heat butter and mustard in large pan, then remove from stove
and toss in bread to coat. Put mixture in buttered 9"x12" baking
dish. Mix cheese and bacon and sprinkle over bread. Beat eggs
and milk and salt and pepper. Pour egg mixture over cheese.
Cover and refrigerate for 24 hours (or overnight). Bake at 325° for
one hour.

Serves 12

*Foothill
House*

**3037 Foothill Boulevard • Calistoga, California 94515
(707) 942-6933**

In a country setting, Foothill House offers spacious rooms individually decorated with antiques, each with private bath and entrance. Queen-size beds, fireplace and small refrigerator. Superior accommodations and attention await guests of Foothill House.

Oven Pancakes

½ c. milk
½ c. flour
3 eggs
1 tsp. sugar
1 tsp. baking soda
Dash salt
2 tart apples (peeled & sliced)
⅓ c. currants
⅓ c. coarsely chopped walnuts
5 Tbsp. butter
½ c. sugar
2 tsp. cinnamon
For variation: Instead of apples, currants, and walnuts, try:
    2 pears (firm), peeled & sliced; ½ c. cranberries, whole;
    1 Tbsp. Gran Marnier

Mix together milk, flour, eggs, sugar, baking soda, and salt until batter is fairly smooth. In a 10-inch oven-proof skillet or deep dish pie plate, saute apples, currants, and walnuts in 3 Tbsp. butter, ¼ c. sugar, and 1 tsp. cinnamon. Pour batter over apples and bake in 400° oven for 10 minutes. Mix together remaining ¼ c. sugar and 1 tsp. cinnamon. Top pancake with sugar/cinnamon mixture and dot with 2 Tbsp. butter. Return to oven until brown and glazed (about 15-20 minutes). Incredible and delicious!

Serves 6

Basil Cheese Torte

5 (8 oz.) pkgs. cream cheese (room temperature)
2 c. basil, fresh
⅔ c. parmesan cheese, freshly grated
⅓ c. olive oil
1 c. pine nuts

Whip four (8 oz.) packages of cream cheese in food processor and set aside. Chop basil in food processor. Add to processor bowl parmesan cheese, olive oil, and remaining package of cream cheese. Mix to blend. Remove from processor and add 1 cup pine nuts. Layer basil spread and plain cream cheese alternately in serving container(s), finishing with the plain cream cheese. Garnish with top of basil stem. Chill 1 hour before serving. Serve with toasted French bread rounds or crackers.

Serves 12 hungry people

Susan's Late Harvest Wine Cake

3 c. flour
1 tsp. baking powder
1 tsp. baking soda
1 tsp. salt
1 tsp. cinnamon
1 tsp. ground cloves

3 eggs
1 c. melted butter
1¾ c. sugar
1 c. Late Harvest Wine
½ c. buttermilk
2 Tbsp. Grand Marnier
4 Tbsp. grated orange rind
1 c. walnuts

Mix together the first 6 ingredients and set aside.

Beat eggs until frothy. Add and mix in remaining ingredients except the orange rind and walnuts.

Add wet to dry ingredients, mix well and add orange rind and walnuts. Pour into greased bundt pan. Bake 350° oven for 50 minutes or until done.

Forest Manor

(707) 965-3538
above Napa Valley

---

415 Cold Springs Road • Angwin, California 94508
(707) 965-3538

Majestic English Tudor estate on 20 secluded acres in the hills above St. Helena in Napa Valley. High vaulted ceilings, massive hand carved beams, fireplaces, decks, pool table, ping pong, suite with private jacuzzi, home baked breakfast.

Gramma's Oatmeal Cookies

3 c. oatmeal, quick
1 c. flour
1 c. sugar
1 tsp. soda (or 3 tsp. baking powder)
1½ tsp. salt
2 tsp. cinnamon
¼ tsp. allspice
¼ c. buttermilk
2 eggs
1 tsp. vanilla
¾ c. oil
½ c. nuts
1 c. dates

Measure oatmeal. Sift in flour, sugar, soda, salt and spices. Mix. Combine liquid ingredients. Mix well and add to dry. Mix all together. Add nuts and dates. Bake 10-12 minutes at 400°.

Yields 4 dozen

Zucchini Bread

3 eggs, beaten
1 c. oil
2¼ c. sugar
2 c. grated zucchini
1 tbsp. vanilla
3 c. flour
1 tbsp. cinnamon
1 tsp. salt
1 tsp. soda
¼ tsp. baking powder
Nuts, raisins or candied fruit (optional)

Beat eggs, add oil, sugar, zucchini and vanilla and mix well. Sift flour, cinnamon, salt, soda and baking powder and fold into liquid mixture. Bake in 2 lb. loaf pan or 2 bread pans for 1 hour at 325°.

Yields 2 loaf pans

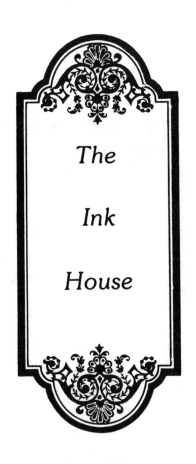

The

Ink

House

1575 St. Helena Hwy. • St. Helena, California 94574
(707) 963-3890

This gracious Italianate Victorian farmhouse built by Theron H. Ink in 1884. Attractions include a porch swing, inviting parlor, complimentary sherry, antique furnishings, four bedrooms with private baths. Continental breakfast and a central valley location. Lois Clark, owner/manager.

155

Aunt Ethel's Date & Raisin Loaf

1 c. chopped dates
1 c. raisins
1 tsp. baking soda
1 tbsp. shortening
2 c. flour
1 egg
½ tsp. salt
½ c. chopped nuts
1 c. white sugar

Pour 1 cup boiling water over fruit and soda. Let cool. Cut shortening into flour. Add beaten egg, salt, nuts and sugar. Fold in fruit. Bake at 370° for 1 hour.   *Yields 1 loaf*

Persimmon Nut Bread

1 c. persimmon pulp
½ tsp. baking soda
1½ c. flour
1 tsp. cinnamon
½ tsp. salt
½ c. chopped walnuts
½ c. raisins

Mix persimmon pulp with baking soda. Combine flour, cinnamon, salt, nuts and raisins. Fold in persimmons. Bake at 325° for 1¼ hours.

Yields 1 loaf

The Inn on Cedar Street

1307 Cedar Street • Calistoga, California 94515
(707) 942-9244

Featured in "PM Magazine," The Inn on Cedar Street is an 1880s
Victorian gingerbread house on a quiet, tree-lined street in Calistoga.
Across the street is the town park, and the inn is two blocks from
downtown Calistoga. Sit in the gazebo or relax on the deck at the rear
of the inn. In the wintertime, hot apple cider is served in the evening; in
the summertime, old-fashioned lemonade, and each night unique bed-
time snacks are put out on the dining table

South of the Border Frittata

16 oz. turkey sausage (hot)
6 eggs
1 c. cream
1½ tsp. baking powder
½ tsp. salt
2 tbsp. flour
6 slices white bread (de-crusted and cubed)
Pepper
1 can (14 oz.) diced chiles
1½ lbs. sharp cheddar, grated
1 tbsp. butter
Sour cream
Avocado (guacamole)
Hot sauce
Tomato wedges

Cook sausage until pink is gone. Set aside. Whisk vigorously eggs and cream. Add baking powder, salt, flour, and bread. Blend. Add a dash of pepper. Lightly butter 2 qt. glass casserole dish. Sprinkle half of the sausage, put half of the chiles on top, then half of the cheese. Add the last half of the sausage, then chiles, then the cheese. Pour egg mixture over top. Dot with butter. Bake at 350° for 40-45 minutes. Let set for 15-20 minutes. Serve in squares with a scoop of sour cream, guacamole, hot sauce, and tomato on top.

Serves 6

Special Good Morning Appetizer

1 lb. dried apricots chopped
2 c. sugar
2 c. apricot nectar
1 tsp. salt
¾ c. shortening
2 bananas mashed
1 jar (small) apricot baby food
2 eggs, beaten
2 tsp. soda
4 c. flour
½ c. chopped pecans
3 bananas
½ c. whipping cream or more if needed

Combine first 5 ingredients. Bring to boil for 5 minutes. Remove apricots. Set aside. Cool liquid, then add bananas, baby food, eggs, soda, flour, and pecans mixing very well. Add reserved apricots. Place in 9"x3" pan or 2 greased, floured loaf pans. Bake at 325° for 45-55 minutes. Put bananas and whipping cream in a blender. Divide in half and fill the middle with whipped bananas and cream. Top with a strawberry.

Serves 12

The Old World Inn

BED AND BREAKFAST

❖

1301 Jefferson Street • Napa, California 94559
(707) 257-0112

❖

Elegant Victorian decorated throughout in bright Swedish colors with coordinated linens and fabrics. Eight bedrooms each with private bathroom. Air-conditioned, large jacuzzi, complimentary wine, international cheeseboard, substantial Continental breakfast and above all a warm welcome.

161

Desperately Healthy Pancakes

½ c. soy flour
½ c. whole wheat flour
½ c. unbleached all-purpose flour
2 tbsp. wheat germ
2 tbsp. powdered milk
2 tbsp. unprocessed bran
1 tbsp. baking powder
½ tsp. baking soda
¼ tsp. salt
Grated peel of 1 orange

2 Eggs separated
½ c. plain yogurt
¼ c. oil
1 tbsp. molasses
1 tbsp. honey
1½ c. orange juice

Mix first 10 ingredients together in a mixer. Separate eggs. Add yokes and all other ingredients to flour mix in processor. Blend well. Beat egg whites stiff. Fold into pancake mixture. Cook on 300° griddle. Cook 2½ minutes one side and 1 minute on the other side. (Look for nice hollow bubbles on first cooking.)

Yields 36 3-inch cakes

Orange Pancake Syrup

2 tbsp. water
¾ c. brown sugar
½ c. concentrated orange juice
¼ lb. butter
1 tbsp. maple flavoring or 2 tbsp. maple syrup
4 tbsp. grated orange peel
½ c. honey

Boil water, sugar, orange concentrate. In processor bowl blend together butter, flavoring, orange peel and honey. Add sugar, orange, water. Mix. Blend well.

Amaretto Torte

Grease 3"x8" layer tins

2 c. sugar
½ c. margarine
½ c. mayonnaise
½ c. Wesson oil
2 eggs
½ c. cocoa
1 c. buttermilk
½ tsp. salt
2 tsp. vanilla
2 tsp. baking soda
2¾ c. all-purpose flour
½ c. amaretto
Walnuts

Preheat oven to 325°

Cream together sugar and margarine. Add mayonnaise and oil, beat thoroughly. Add eggs and beat. Add cocoa. Mix, slowly adding buttermilk. Add salt, vanilla, baking soda and flour. Mix well. Add 1 c. boiling water. Fill 3 cake tins equally. Bake 35 minutes at 325° or until done. Remove from pans and cool. Wrap in Saran Wrap and freeze until ready to use. Remove from freezer and slice through in frozen state. Sprinkle on both halves ½ c. amaretto. Spread chocolate icing (recipe follows) and replace top half. Spread chococlate icing on top of cake and decorate with half walnuts.

Easily adapted for food processor.

Yields 3x8" layers

Chocolate Icing

1 pint heavy whipping cream
20 oz. good quality cooking chocolate

In pan, bring cream to a boil. Remove from heat and stir in chocolate. Stir until smooth icing forms. (This can be done in a food processor.) This icing will keep in a refrigerator for a month or so.

Buttermilk and Mushroom Crepes

BUTTERMILK CREPES:
2 Eggs
1 c. buttermilk
2 tbsp. oil
⅓ c. water
½ c. sifted cake flour
½ c. all-purpose flour
½ tsp. salt

Blend all ingredients, cook as regular crepes.

Yields 14-16 6" crepes

MUSHROOM CREPES:
½ lb. butter
1 lb. fresh mushrooms, finely chopped
¼ c. minced green onions
1 c. minced ham
Black pepper (quite a lot)
2 oz. slivered almonds
1 c. sour cream
8 buttermilk crepes

Melt butter in large saucepan. Add mushrooms and onions. Saute over high heat 4-5 minutes until dry. Add ham and pepper. Cook over moderate heat for quite a long time until most of liquid is absorbed. Stir in almonds. Cool. Just before filling crepes, stir in sour cream. Fill crepes and fold crepe around filling. For luncheon dish, serve with cheese or mustard sauce.

Oliver House

Bed and Breakfast Country Inn

2970 Silverado Trail • St. Helena, California 94574
(707) 963-4089

Warm, intimate country atmosphere. Picturesque Swiss Chalet overlooking acres of vineyards. Private baths and fireplaces. French doors open onto balconies with view. Scrumptious breakfast served in the cozy country kitchen. Eight wineries within walking distance.

Granola Crunch with an Oliver Twist

4 fresh grapefruit
2 c. crushed cornflakes
½ c. brown sugar
2 tbsp. butter
⅓ c. honey
¼ c. walnuts
¼ c. pecans
1 tsp. cinnamon

Halve grapefruit and loosen sections from membrane. Combine remaining ingredients; sprinkle 2 tablespoons of the mixture evenly over top of each half. Broil fruit until topping is golden brown. Serve immediately. Makes 8 servings. You will have topping left over which can be stored in air tight container. Other uses are:

- Topping over fruit salad.
- Mix into waffle batter ½ cup.
- Sprinkle over ice cream.
- As a spread on toast or bread, combine ¼ cup of topping mix with ½ cup of honey and ½ cup of peanut butter.

Serves 8

Swiss Summer Salad

2 lbs. fresh ripe garden tomatoes
Juice of 2 lemons squeezed fresh
¼ c. of salad oil
Salt and pepper

Place tomatoes in boiling water for 2 minutes until skin peels off easily. Skin tomatoes and cut into small sections and place in large bowl. Pour fresh lemon juice over tomatoes and mix in salad oil gently. Salt and pepper to taste and refrigerate for 30 minutes to 1 hour allowing tomatoes to blend with flavors of lemon juice and seasonings.

Serves 4

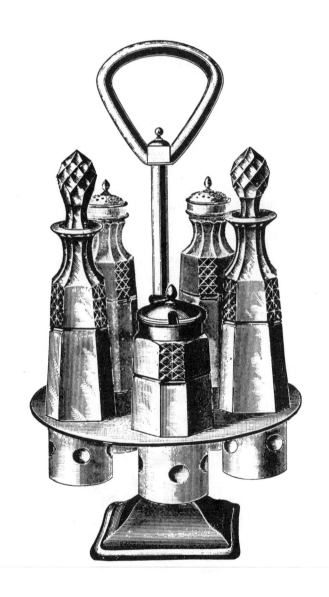

Scarlett's Country Inn

M. Fischer

---❖---

3918 Silverado Trail • Calistoga, California 94515
(707) 942-6669

---❖---

Secluded French country farmhouse close to spas and wineries.
Breakfast served by woodland pool.

171

Scarlett's French Toast

6 fresh eggs
½ c. buttermilk
1 tsp. vanilla
6 slices thick white bread
Cinnamon
Powdered sugar

Beat the eggs with a wire whip together with buttermilk and vanilla. Dip pieces of thick white bread in mixture, coating both sides. Put on medium hot, buttered griddle. Add an additional tablespoon of mixture on each piece, pricking with fork to let it soak in. Sprinkle with cinnamon. Turn when bottom is browned. Serve with a sprinkle of powdered sugar.

Serves 2

Shrimp & Rice Curry Salad

2 c. cooked rice
¼ c. finely chopped onion
½ tsp. curry powder
1½ tbsp. white vinegar
2 tbsp. salad oil
1 c. finely chopped celery
¼ c. finely chopped green pepper
¾ c. mayonnaise
2 cans tiny shrimp

Marinate rice, onion, and curry powder in vinegar and oil while chopping vegetables. Add remaining ingredients, except shrimp. Mix well and chill 2 hours before serving or make 2 days ahead, adding shrimp just before serving. This is a great cold rice salad for summer picnics.

Serves 6

Marinated Shrimp & Bay Scallops

1 lb. of fresh or frozen bay scallops thawed
    (Sea scallops can be used, cut into halves or quarters)
¾ c. lime juice
¾ lb. fresh or frozen, shelled, deveined shrimp thawed
½ avocado, peeled, pitted and coarsely chopped
¼ c. finely chopped onion
1½ tbsp. olive oil
1 tbsp. minced fresh or 2 tsp. crushed dried coriander leaves

Place uncooked scallops in glass baking dish or bowl; pour lime juice over. Let stand covered 1 hour. Stir in uncooked shrimp, chopped avocado, onion, olive oil, and coriander; refrigerate covered 8 hours or overnight. Spoon scallops mixture into serving dish. Garnish with lime slices.

Serves 6

Villa St. Helena

2727 Sulphur Springs Avenue • St. Helena, California 94574
(707) 963-2514

Secluded hilltop Mediterranean Villa combining quiet country elegance with panoramic views of Napa Valley. Romantic, antique filled rooms. Private entrances, baths, some fireplaces. A private world on wooded 20-acre estate. Walking trails, spacious courtyard, pool. Tennis nearby. Complimentary wine. Continental breakfast. Visa, MasterCard, American Express.

Pecan Tea Cakes

2 eggs
1 c. brown sugar
½ c. all-purpose flour
½ tsp. baking powder
Salt, pinch
1 c. chopped pecans

Beat eggs well. Add sugar and flour which has been sifted with baking powder and salt. Add chopped pecans. Bake in tiny muffin pans in moderate (350°) oven for 20 minutes.

Cheese Apple Crisp

1½ qt. apples, peeled and sliced
1 stick cinnamon
¾ c. water
1 c. white wine
¾ c. sugar, granulated
1 c. all-purpose flour
⅓ tsp. salt
¼ lb. butter
6 oz. grated cheddar cheese (sharp)

Place apples in sauce pot with cinnamon, water, white wine, and sugar. Poach until tender. Drain, reserving 1 cup of the poaching liquid. Place apples in shallow greased baking dish. Pour on reserved poaching liquid. Combine sugar, flour and salt; work in the butter to form a crumbly mixture. Lightly stir in the cheese. Spread mixture over apples and bake in oven at 350° until the crust is brown and crisp.

SACRAMENTO

B&B

BED AND BREAKFAST

INNS

- •Amber House
- •Aunt Abigail's
- •Bear Flag Inn
- •Briggs House
- •Driver Mansion Inn

Sacramento was once a center of civilization for weary miners during the Gold Rush days of the mid to late 1800s. History can be relived in this river city by visits to Old Sacramento, the famous Railroad Museum, recently restored State Capitol, Governor's Mansion, Crocker Art Museum, and Sutter's Fort.

Today the Capital City serves as both the legislative center for the most populous state in the union and transportation center for the great Central Valley, one of the most productive agricultural regions on earth. The waterways system of the Sacramento and American Rivers provide exhilirating rapids for rafting to the east, and lazy delta for houseboating to the west, as well as one of the nation's finest bicycle trails along its banks. The Convention Center and Theater offer special events, exhibits and entertainment, including the Sacramento Symphony and Ballet.

The Bed and Breakfast Inns of Sacramento extend the historical richness of their restored vintage homes—from classic pillared Victorians to craftsman bungalows—along with modern day comfort, hospitality, and scrumptious breakfasts to business guests, tourists, and seekers of romance alike.

Amber House

1315 22nd Street • Sacramento, California 95816
(916) 444-8085

Enjoy the tailored elegance of this 1905 Craftsman—boxed beam alderwood ceilings, leaded glass windows and bookcases, oriental rugs, English antiques. Sit beside the fireplace with a glass of wine. A short walk from the State Capitol.

Chocolate Coffeecake

6 tbsp. butter
½ c. sugar
2 eggs
½ tsp. vanilla
¼ c. sour cream
1½ c. flour
1 tsp. baking powder
½ tsp. soda
½ c. orange juice
1-2 tsp. grated orange peel
Chocolate streusel (recipe follows)
½ c. semi-sweet chocolate chips

Cream butter and sugar in large mixer bowl. Add eggs and vanilla and beat well. Blend in sour cream. Combine flour, baking powder and soda in small bowl. Add to batter mixture alternately with orange juice, blending well. Stir in peel.

Pour half of batter into greased 9 inch square pan. Sprinkle half of Chocolate Streusel evenly over batter. Spoon remaining batter into pan and spread evenly to cover streusel. Sprinkle remaining streusel over top. Bake at 350° for 30 minutes or until cake tester inserted in center comes out clean. Sprinkle with chocolate chips. Serve warm or cold.

Serves 10

Chocolate Streusel

⅔ c. brown sugar, packed
½ c. chopped walnuts
½ c. semisweet chocolate chips

Combine sugar and walnuts. Divide mixture in half.

Sprinkle chocolate chips on one-half of streusel mixture.

Crab Custard Casserole

¼ c. (½ cube) butter or margarine, melted
12 eggs
½ c. milk
1 tsp. salt
½ tsp. white pepper
½ tsp. dillweed
1 c. fresh or canned crabmeat
8 oz. cream cheese, cut into small cubes
Paprika

Pour melted butter into an 8-inch square baking pan; spread butter to coat bottom of pan. Beat eggs, milk, salt, pepper and dillweed. Stir in crabmeat and cheese cubes. Pour mixture into pan. Cover with plastic wrap or aluminum foil and refrigerate overnight or up to 24 hours. Uncover pan, sprinkle with paprika and bake at 350° for 40-45 minutes or until center is set.

Serves 6-8

Aunt Abigail's Bed & Breakfast

2120 G Street • Sacramento, California 95816
(916) 441-5007

1912 colonial revival mansion, light and airy. Five individually decorated guest rooms. Full breakfasts. Our guests say: "You have a wonderful gift of service, hospitality, caring, and are a great cook! Thanks, especially for all the extra touches."

Super Cinners

2 c. sifted flour
3 tsp. baking powder
2 tbsp. cinnamon
¼ tsp. salt
2 eggs
1 c. milk
½ c. salad oil
1 c. brown sugar, firmly packed
1 c. chopped nuts
1 c. raisins

In a mixing bowl, sift flour again with baking powder, cinnamon and salt. Beat eggs slightly, stir in milk, salad oil and brown sugar. Add to dry ingredients all at once and mix quickly. Stir in nuts and raisins. Spoon into 12 muffin cups and bake in a 375° oven for 12-15 minutes.

Serves 12

Peach/Pear Bake

1 can (16 oz.) peach halves
1 can (16 oz.) pear halves
2 tbsp. cornstarch
1 tsp. pumpkin pie spice
½ c. firmly packed brown sugar
½ c. flour
¼ c. (½ stick) butter
½ c. walnuts

Drain syrup from fruit into a small saucepan. Half pears and peaches and place in shallow baking dish (pie pan works nicely). Stir cornstarch and pumpkin pie spice into syrups in saucepan until smooth. Cook, stirring constantly until mixture thickens and bubbles. Pour over fruits in baking dish.

Combine brown sugar, flour and nuts in a small bowl. Cut in butter until mixture is well blended. Spread on fruit. Bake in 375° for 30 minutes or until top is golden. Serve with a dollop of freshly whipped cream.

Serves 6-8

Chili Cheese Strata

12 slices of white bread, cubed
2½ c. grated monterey jack cheese
1 4-oz can chiles, diced
6 eggs
2½ c. milk
½ c. salsa
Salt and pepper to taste

Butter a pie pan. Layer ½ bread and ½ cheese, sprinkle chiles over top. (For milder taste, use only ½ can.) Place second layer of bread cubes and cheese on top. Mix eggs, salsa and seasonings. Pour over bread, cheese and chiles. Cover and refrigerate overnight. Preheat oven to 350°. Bake 50-60 minutes until golden and firm in center.

Serves 8

Bear Flag Inn

2814 I Street • Sacramento, California 95816
(916) 448-5417

Located in Sacramento's historic midtown district, Bear Flag Inn offers an ideal setting for nurturing a romance, plotting an adventure or for simply hanging one's hat at the end of a day's work.

187

Sweet Strata

10-12 slices of white bread
3 eggs
2 c. Half & Half
1 tsp. vanilla
½ c. sugar
Dash of nutmeg

FILLING:
12 oz. cream cheese
1 tsp. vanilla
1 egg
⅓ c. sugar

Trim crusts from bread. Arrange ½ of the bread in greased 1½ quart casserole dish or souffle dish so that bread covers the entire bottom of dish. In separate bowl, mix eggs, Half & Half, vanilla, and sugar. Pour ½ of this liquid over bread. In another bowl, beat all of filling ingredients together until creamy. Pour filling over moistened bread. Arrange the other ½ of bread over the top of cheese filling and pour the rest of the egg mixture over the top. Sprinkle top with dash of nutmeg. Let stand in the refrigerator overnight. Bake in covered dish in oven pre-heated to 350° for 30 minutes, then remove cover and bake for another 20 minutes until puffy. Let stand 10 minutes before serving.

Serves 4

(May be served topped with hot apple butter, warm fruit of the season, or carmel sauce.)

Sausage-Leek Quiche

¼ lb. spicy ground sausage
1 leek sliced thin
1 pastry crust
1½ c. jack cheese, grated*
3 eggs
2 c. Half & Half

Saute sausage until half done, then add leek. Continue to saute until both sausage and leek are completely cooked. Prepare pastry crust. Toss sausage, leek, and cheese together and place in pastry crust. In separate bowl, mix eggs and Half & Half. Pour egg mixture over ingredients in pastry crust. Bake in oven preheated to 375° for 45-55 minutes until top is brown.

---

*More or less cheese may be used according to taste. If increasing the amount of cheese, decrease the amount of Half & Half.

Serves 4-6

2209 Capitol Avenue • Sacramento, California 95816
(916) 441-3214

Comfort, friendliness, and pampered service in this elegant yet homelike 1901 Colonial Revival near the State Capitol. Seven guest rooms in main house and secluded carriage house, gourmet breakfast, fireplaces, sauna, spa, bicycles, garden, walking distance to fine dining.

Potato Jumble

4 potatoes, pre-baked with skin on, diced in ½" chunks
¾ c. onion
2 c. vegetables (assorted colors such as mushrooms, squash, peppers, tomatoes)
½ tsp. salt
¼ tsp. pepper
2 tbsp. parsley, chopped
¼ tsp. paprika
¼ tsp. garlic powder
4 tbsp. butter
1 c. sharp cheddar cheese, grated
¼ c. sour cream

Saute potatoes, vegetables, and seasonings in butter until potatoes are browned. Top with cheese. Cover until cheese is melted. Garnish with sour cream.

Serves 4

Fiesta Delight

6 eggs beaten slightly
1 lb. jack cheese, grated
1 pt. farmer style cottage cheese
1 4 oz. can chopped jalapena peppers
1 c. Bisquick
1 c. milk
1 cube butter, melted

Mix all above ingredients in a large bowl. Pour into a 9"x13" pyrex baking dish. Bake at 350° for 40 minutes. Top will be golden brown. Wait a few minutes before serving.

Serves 8

Eggs Florentine Solo Style

Butter
1 tbsp. chopped, steamed spinach
1 tsp. parmesan cheese
1 egg
1 tbsp. heavy cream
1 tsp. parmesan cheese

Preheat oven to 350°. Butter individual ramekins. Put chopped spinach in bottom topped with cheese. Break one large egg into each. Cover with heavy cream. Sprinkle with cheese. Bake 8-10 minutes or until egg is set.

Individual Serving

Poached Pears with Almonds

4 underripe Anjou or Bosc pears
½ c. sugar
¼ c. orange juice
2 tbsp. lemon juice
2 tsp. grated lemon rind
1 slice fresh ginger root or ½ tsp. ground ginger
¼ c. blanched almonds, split and toasted
Top with whipped cream or creme fraiche

Peel pears and cut out blossom end. Don't remove the stem. In deep saucepan mix sugar, orange juice, lemon juice, lemon rind and ginger. Bring to boiling. Place pears in syrup. Bring to boiling again. Cover and simmer 25-30 minutes or until pears are tender when pierced with a fork. Arrange pears in deep serving dish. Pour syrup over top. Sprinkle with almonds. Serve slightly warm or chilled with whipped cream or creme fraiche if desired.

Serves 8

THE DRIVER MANSION INN

2019 Twenty-First Street • Sacramento, California 95818
(916) 455-5243

Grand 1899 Victorian Mansion featuring large, exquisitely appointed rooms, spacious gardens and uniquely renovated carriage house with spas, fireplaces and skylights. Warm, elegant, cheerful. Sumptuous breakfast included.

Anily's Banana Nut Bread

½ c. cooking oil
1 c. sugar
2 eggs
3 ripe bananas, mashed
3 tbsp. milk
2 c. flour
1 tsp. baking soda
½ tsp. baking powder
½ tsp. salt
½ tsp. vanilla
1 c. broken walnuts

Beat first five ingredients together in large mixing bowl. Add sifted dry ingredients and mix. Add vanilla nuts and mix. Pour into 1 greased and floured loaf pan. Bake at 350° for 60-80 minutes. Cool well and store overnight before cutting.

Serves 10-12

Cheese Blintzes

CREPES:
2 eggs
1 c. milk
¾ c. flour
Pinch salt
1 tbsp. oil
Butter for frying

Blend first five ingredients well. Melt one tsp. butter in 7" frying pan. Add just enough batter to cover bottom of pan. Fry on one side only until lightly browned and cooked through. Remove from pan and continue to use up batter adding a little butter when necessary.

FILLING:
2 c. ricotta cheese
2 tbsp. sugar
1 egg
½ tsp. vanilla

Blend all four ingredients well. Put a generous spoonful of filling on each crepe (on browned side). Roll up and fry in butter until cooked through and golden brown. Serve two or three on each plate topped with jam or fruit and a dollop of sour cream.

Serves 6-8

SAN FRANCISCO BAY AREA INNS

- Albion House
- The Inn San Francisco
- Lord Bradley's Inn
- The Monte Cristo
- The Spreckels Mansion
- Victorian Inn on the Park

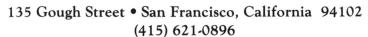

135 Gough Street • San Francisco, California 94102
(415) 621-0896

Tucked away behind Symphony Hall, offering a memorable stay in rooms filled with antiques. Large, elegant, living room comfortably accommodates receptions of 50-100. Private baths, suites.

Key Lime Pie

4 eggs (yolks)
1 15-oz. can of sweetened condensed milk
¼ c. Key Lime Juice (or regular fresh lime juice)
1 graham cracker crust
4 egg whites
¼ c. sugar

Beat the egg yolks and slowly stir in the condensed milk. Add the lime juice and stir well. When the mixture resembles pudding pour it into the shell. Bake the pie in a 350° oven for about 10-15 minutes until the filling is firm. Allow to cool for 20 minutes. Meanwhile beat the egg whites and sugar until the egg whites are firm. Scoop this mixture onto the top of the pie and spread around like a frosting. Place into a 450° oven and bake for about 10 more minutes until the top is just lightly browned.

Pasta Salad

1 bag pasta shells
1 c. vinaigrette dressing
1 can tuna
1 small can olives
4 oz. slivered almonds
1 green pepper diced

Boil the pasta for 6-8 minutes in boiling salted water with just a little oil. Drain and cool. Stir in the rest of the ingredients. (Good Seasons Italian Dressing works well with this.)

Serves 4-5

Southern Style Pecan Pie

3 eggs
1 c. chopped pecans
1 c. brown sugar
¼ c. corn syrup
¼ tsp. salt
¼ c. dark rum
4 tbsp. melted butter

1 unbaked pie shell

Beat the eggs thoroughly, then add all of the other ingredients
and stir until all of the sugar is dissolved. Pour into the pie shell
and bake for 40-45 minutes in a 375° oven until the filling is firm.
Serve with whipped cream or vanilla ice cream.

Serves 8-10

---

943 South Van Ness Ave. • San Francisco, California 94110
(415) 641-0188

Comfort and hospitality in a gracious 1878 mansion. Splendid Victoriana, antiques, fresh flowers. Sun deck and hot tub. A most affordable luxury accommodation. Parking available.

Soft Gingerbread

1 c. butter
1 c. honey
2 tsp. baking soda dissolved in 1 c. boiling water
1 c. molasses
1 tsp. salt
1 tsp. ginger
1 tsp. cinnamon
2¾ c. unbleached white flour
2 eggs

Cream together butter and honey. Then add next 7 ingredients. Mix all well, then beat in eggs. Pour in 9"x13" well oiled baking dish. Bake at 350° for 45 minutes. Serve with whipped cream.

Serves 6-8

Apple Nut Cake

3 eggs
2 c. sugar
1¼ c. oil
1 tsp. vanilla
3 c. chopped apples
1 tsp. salt
1 tsp. soda
3 c. flour
1 c. chopped pecans

Beat eggs well; add sugar, oil and vanilla. Mix well. Add apples. Sift salt and soda with flour. Add apple batter to flour; add nuts and blend well. Bake in 2 greased 9-inch layer pans starting in a cold oven set at 325°. Bake for 45 minutes. Serve with a generous dollop of fresh whipped cream.

Serves 6-8

Refrigerator Rolls

1 c. shortening
¾ c. sugar
1 c. boiling water
2 pkg. dry yeast or yeast cakes
1 c. warm water
2 eggs well beaten
6 c. flour
1 tsp. salt

Cream shortening; add sugar. Add boiling water and stir until sugar and shortening are dissolved. Cool. Dissolve yeast in warm water. Add to above mixture. Blend well. Add well beaten eggs; sift flour and salt and add to mixture. Cover and place in refrigerator overnight. When ready to use, place small portions of dough which have been kneaded in your hands in well greased muffin tins. Fill ⅓ full. Let rise in warm place covered for 2 hours and bake at 400° for 15 minutes. A very light delicious roll.

Yields 36

Lord Bradley's Inn

43344 Mission Boulevard • Fremont, California 94539
(415) 490-0520

Enjoy the comforts of our Victorian home nestled among rolling foothills. Your choice of eight rooms, all with private baths, furnished in antiques and named after family members.

Anne McMuffins

1 bunch green onions, chopped
1 lb. shredded, sharp cheddar cheese
1 can chopped black olives
1 c. mayonnaise
2 tsp. curry powder
1 pkg. sourdough English muffins

Mix onions, cheese, olives, mayonnaise and curry in a bowl. Spread on English muffins. Bake at 350° for 10 minutes or until bubbly. Can be served whole or cut in fourths. Mixture will last at least five days in the refrigerator. Serve for afternoon or evening refreshments.

Serves 20

Sir Keith's French Toast

4 eggs
1 c. milk
½ tsp. cinnamon
1 tsp. vanilla
8 oz. cream cheese
1 loaf sliced, sour French bread
1 c. marmalade
Powdered sugar

Beat eggs until frothy, add milk, cinnamon and vanilla. Set aside. Spread soft creamed cheese on one side of French bread. Spread marmalade on one side of cheese covered bread. Put two slices together, cheese inside. Dip in egg mixture. Cook on griddle until brown on both sides. Sprinkle with powdered sugar. Serve with Orange Butter.

NOTE: Cheese should be spread completely over bread to edge of crust so that a good seal can be made, and no egg batter is inside.

Serves 8

Orange Butter

8 oz. cream cheese
½ lb. margarine
1 lb. powdered sugar
1 small can frozen orange juice, thawed

Beat well. Can be frozen until ready to use.

Lady Donna's Cream Scones

1 c. buttermilk
1 egg
2 tbsp. sugar
3½ c. unbleached white flour
2 tsp. baking powder
1 tsp. baking soda
½ c. melted butter
¾ c. raisins

Beat together buttermilk, egg and sugar. In separate bowl, mix 3 cups flour, baking soda and baking powder. Add about ⅔ of flour mixture to buttermilk mixture and stir well. Gradually add melted butter, mixing thoroughly. Stir in remaining flour and raisins. Add additional flour if needed to make a stiff dough. Turn dough on lightly floured board, knead for several minutes. Separate dough into 3 equal parts. Shape each part in a thick circle. Flatten each circle slightly. Cut into quarters. Arrange on lightly buttered baking sheet. Bake at 400° for 20-25 minutes or until lightly browned.

For variety, you can add grated lemon rind or a couple of mashed bananas.

Serves 12

The MONTE CRISTO

600 Presidio Avenue • San Francisco, California 94115
(415) 931-1875

Reflecting San Francisco's cultural diversity, including a Chinese wedding bed in the Oriental Room, and a canopied fourposter in the Georgian Room—particular favorites of honeymooners. Private and shared baths.

213

Gooseberry Pancakes

⅔ c. oatmeal
1⅓ c. whole wheat flour
⅔ c. yellow cornmeal
⅔ c. all-purpose flour
4 tsp. baking powder
2 tsp. baking soda
2 tsp. salt
¾ c. cold butter
4 c. buttermilk
4 eggs
⅓ c. maple syrup
2 c. cooked or canned gooseberries

Grind oatmeal to powder. Add whole wheat flour, yellow corn meal, all-purpose flour, baking powder, baking soda and salt. Blend in cold butter, cut into bits until mix resembles meal. Combine buttermilk, lightly beaten eggs and maple syrup in a bowl. Add liquid to dry mixture. Let batter stand 5 minutes. Thin with buttermilk if too thick. Cook on preheated, moderately hot griddle or pan. Add heated gooseberries to top of pancakes before serving.

Serves 8

Whole Wheat Bread

6 c. body temperature water
3 tbsp. yeast
1 c. honey
5 c. white flour
3 tbsp. salt
1 c. oil
10-13 c. whole wheat flour

Combine water, yeast and honey. Let sit 5 minutes. Add white flour. Let sit 20 minutes. Add salt, oil and mix. Add whole wheat flour until it forms a ball. Roll on floured surface. Add more flour as needed so it's not sticky. Knead for 10 minutes. Let rest in a covered bowl for 1 hour in a warm spot in the kitchen. Butter bread pans. Cut bread into five equal parts. Bake at 350° for 1-1½ hours. Mmmmmm, delicious!

Yields 5 loaves

the
Spreckels Mansion

---❖---

**737 Buena Vista West • San Francisco, California 94117
(415) 861-3008**

---❖---

*Awarded the "Best Bed and Breakfast Inn in San Francisco" by the
S.F. Bay Guardian newspaper. Past guests agree and we are sure you
will too.*

Pate de le Pape

2 large yellow onions, coarsely chopped
Olive oil
2 lbs. chicken livers (fat removed)
¼ tsp. Cinzano or Madera wine
1 tbsp. Italian seasoning
1/8 tsp. cayenne pepper
1 tbsp. soy sauce
¼ lb. unsalted butter, cut in pats

In a heavy 10" skillet, saute onions in olive oil until deep golden
brown (very important). Add chicken livers and saute until
brown, with a little pink inside. Add Cinzano or Madera and stir.
Stir in Italian seasoning, cayenne, soy sauce. Remove from heat,
cool slightly.

In a strong blender or processor with a metal blade, combine
livers with butter, a pat at a time, until very smooth. Pour into an
attractive serving dish and chill. This is a lovely, easy to make
pate for your hors d'oeuvre tray.

10 Minute Stir-Fry

1 chicken breast
1 pork steak
1 beef steak
Prawns

Select one or none of the above meats. If no meat is used, add another vegetable. Cut meat (approximately ½ lb.) into thin bite-sized slices.

2 tbsp. oil
1 bunch green onions, sliced diagonally into 1" lengths
1 clove garlic, sliced thin (optional)
2 tbsp. olive oil

1 red pepper, in chunks
1 zucchini, sliced
1 summer squash, in chunks
A handful of snow peas
1 tomato, halved and quartered
2 stalks of bok choy, sliced   2 tbsp. oyster sauce
1 stalk broccoli, sliced   ¼ tsp. black bean sauce
4 asparagus, chopped in 1" pieces   1 dash of curry (optional)
                                      1 tbsp. soy sauce
Select 4 of the above vegetables.

Saute meat in 2 tbsp. oil over high heat until barely brown. Add green onion and garlic. Don't overcook. Transfer to a bowl. In the same pan, add oil and stir-fry the vegetables until ½ done (still crispy). Return meat to pan. Stir in oyster and bean sauces. Add curry powder if desired. Remove from heat. Stir in soy sauce. Serve over rice. If you want to be really nutritious, use long grain brown rice, but white rice is good as well.

---

301 Lyon Street • San Francisco, California 94117
(415) 931-1830

A San Francisco Historical landmark. Enjoy romance in this faithfully restored Victorian mansion. Large dining room, parlour. The perfect getaway spot. Fireplaces, private baths, views.

Blueberry Bread

2 c. sugar
3 c. flour
1½ tsp. soda
1 tbsp. cinnamon
1 tsp. salt
2 baskets of blueberries
    (Can substitute two 10-oz. pkg. frozen strawberries, drained,
    or blackberries or fresh strawberries.)
1¼ c. oil
4 eggs beaten

Mix all dry ingredients. Make well in center and pour all liquid
ingredients into well. Mix by hand. Grease and flour 2 bread pans
(8"x4") and bake for one hour at 350° or until done.

Serves 25

Bran Muffins

5 c. flour (2½ c. whole wheat flour plus 2½ c. white flour)
5 tsp. soda
2 tsp. salt
3 c. flour

4 beaten eggs
1 c. melted shortening
1 qt. buttermilk
1 — 15 oz. box raisin bran

Combine all of the above ingredients except raisin bran. Mix well and add raisin bran. Mix well. (This takes a very large bowl.) Pour into greased muffin pan ⅔ full.   Bake at 400° for 15 minutes or until done. Add raisins, drained pineapple, chopped dates or nuts if desired.

Serves 48 plus

SANTA CRUZ, HALF MOON BAY, MONTEREY PENINSULA INNS

- Apple Lane Inn
- Babbling Brook Inn
- Cliff Crest Inn
- Mangels House
- Mill Rose Inn
- New Davenport
- Rancho San Gregorio
- Seven Gables Inn

6265 Soquel Drive • Aptos, California 95003
(408) 475-6868

Victorian farm house overlooking Monterey Bay. Quiet and secluded. Beaches, redwoods, wineries, and restaurants nearby. Elegant period parlor with travertine fireplace. Library on geography, exploration and travel. Five guest rooms.

Coddled Eggs

1 pat of butter (1/8 tsp.)
½ tsp. cream
1 tbsp. diced ham
1 tbsp. diced cheddar cheese
1 egg
¼ tsp. thyme or dillweed

Put into egg coddler in following order: butter, cream, most of the ham and cheese, egg, remaining ham and cheese. Sprinkle seasoning on top. Immerse egg coddler into boiling water (about ¾ of egg coddler). Cover and boil 10 to 12 minutes. Make sure cap is *not* screwed on tightly.

Individual Servings

Spicy Apple Muffins

1½ c. flour
¾ c. sugar
1¾ tsp. baking powder
½ tsp. salt
½ tsp. cardamon
½ c. butter
1 egg
¼ c. milk
1 c. grated apples
¾ c. chopped walnuts
¼ c. melted butter
1 tsp. cinnamon combined with
   ¼ c. sugar

Mix flour, sugar, baking powder, salt, and cardamon. Cut in butter until crumbly. Mix in egg and milk. Fold in grated apples and walnuts. Fill muffin cup ¼ full. Brush on melted butter and sprinkle with sugar/cinnamon. Bake 20-25 minutes at 350°.

Eggs Pierre

18 eggs
10 slices sour dough French bread
Butter
Pinch or 2 thyme
Dash cayenne
10 slices cheddar cheese
10 slices ham
10 slices Swiss cheese
⅓ c. cream
Garlic salt
Medium grain black pepper
Worcestershire sauce—dash or 2

The Day Before:

Butter 10"x19" Pyrex dish. Arrange buttered French bread and layer with cheddar, ham, and Swiss cheese. Mix other ingredients in bowl and whisk with whip 2-3 minutes. Pour over layered ham and cheeses. Cover with wrap. Put in refrigerator overnight. Remove an hour before breakfast. Preheat oven to 350°-375°. Sprinkle with grated ham and cheeses. Bake 20-25 minutes. Top will be crispy. Serve bubbly.

The Babbling Brook Inn

1025 Laurel Street • Santa Cruz, California 95060
(408) 427-2437

Twelve rooms with country French decor. Private baths, phones, fire-places, and televisions available. Laurel Creek flows by your private deck and through beautifully landscaped gardens. Walking distance to beach, boardwalk and downtown. Complimentary wine and sherry and sumptuous continental breakfast.

231

Texas Pookie Muffins

1 c. flour
1 c. whole wheat flour
¾ c. sugar
2 tsp. baking soda
2 tsp. ground cinnamon
½ tsp. salt
1½ c. shredded carrots
1½ c. shredded apples
¾ c. coconut
½ c. snipped dates
½ c. chopped nuts
3 beaten eggs
½ c. oil
½ c. buttermilk
1 tsp. vanilla

Combine dry ingredients in large bowl. Combine carrot, apple, coconut, dates, and nuts in another bowl. Combine eggs, oil, buttermilk and vanilla and add to fruit-nut mixture. Stir into dry ingredients. (Do not overmix.) Spoon batter into greased muffin pans lined with paper cups or sprayed with non-stick pan coating. Bake at 375° 15 to 18 minutes. Remove from oven when golden and they spring back. Let cool on wire rack.

Yields 24 Muffins

Fruit & Cheese Danish

8 oz. cream cheese softened
3 eggs beaten
3 tbsp. flour
6 tbsp. sugar
1 pie crust
Peach or apricot preserves
Sliced fresh peaches, apples or apricots
Sliced almonds

Soften cream cheese (or substitute 8 oz. of low-fat cottage cheese smoothed in the blender for a lower calorie recipe). Add eggs together with flour and sugar. Roll out pastry to fit small size jelly roll pan and flute edges. Bake 5 minutes at 425°, cool slightly and cover with egg and cheese mixture. Cover with topping of peach or apricot preserves and sliced fresh peaches, apples, or apricots, and sprinkle with sliced almonds. Bake about 20 minutes at 375° or until custard filling is set. Cool slightly and cut into squares.

Yields 32 pieces

Imitation Crab Mini Quiche

1 pie crust
½ lb. imitation crab meat
1 c. monterey jack, Swiss or mozzarella cheese
⅓ c. green onions
4 eggs
2 c. Half & Half
1 tbsp. minced parsley
½ tsp. salt
1/8 tsp. red pepper

Pastry for 9" pie, makes 12 mini quiches (double for 24). Roll out pastry and cut in circles with tea cup and shape to fit in muffin tins. Prick bottoms and bake at 425° for 5 minutes. Cool.

Flake imitation crab (you can also use ham) and divide into pastry lined muffin tin. Grate cheese and sprinkle over crab meat. Add minced green onions. Beat eggs with Half & Half, add minced green parsley, salt, red pepper; and pour over crabmeat mixture. Bake at 325° for about 20 minutes or until set. Let stand 10 minutes before trying to remove from pans. Serve with fresh sprigs of parsley.

Yields 12 mini quiches

CLIFF CREST

---❧---

407 Cliff Street • Santa Cruz, California 95060
(408) 427-2609

---❧---

Pampered elegance in a romantic Victorian mansion. Five rooms, all with private bathrooms, antiques, and fresh flowers. Complimentary breakfast served in bed or garden solarium. Located on one-half acre lush grounds and gardens, one and a half blocks from beach.

235

Fresh Cranberry Orange Muffins

1 egg
2 c. flour
½ tsp. baking soda
¼ tsp. salt
½ c. sugar
2 tbsp. orange juice
2 tbsp. oil
1 c. pureed orange, peel and all (place whole orange into food
    processor)
¼ c. chopped cranberry

Heat oven to 400°. Line 10 muffin cups with paper baking cups.
Beat egg slightly; stir in remaining ingredients just until
moistened. Divide batter evenly among cups. Bake 15 minutes or
until golden brown.

Serves 10

Cinnamon Applesauce Muffins

¼ c. granulated sugar
1 tsp. cinnamon

1 egg
2 c. flour
½ tsp. baking soda
¼ tsp. salt
¾ c. applesauce
⅓ c. brown sugar
2 tbsp. vegetable oil
½ tsp. cinnamon
¼ tsp. nutmeg
¼ tsp. allspice
4 tbsp. melted butter

Heat oven to 450°. Line ten muffin cups with paper baking cups. Mix granulated sugar with 1 tsp. cinnamon and reserve. Mix remaining ingredients except butter with fork just until moistened. Divide batter among muffin cups. Bake 15 minutes or until golden brown. While warm dip tops into melted butter, then into sugar-cinnamon mixture.

Yields 10

Baked Apples

10 Granny Smith apples
10 tsp. brown sugar
10 tsp. butter
5 tsp. cinnamon
⅓ c. water

Peel top half and core apples. Place in baking pan. Place 1 tsp. brown sugar, 1 tsp. butter and ½ cinnamon into empty cores. Pour ⅓ c. water into pan. Bake at 350° for 40 to 45 minutes, occasionally spooning bubbling syrup at bottom of pan over apples. Serve hot.

Serves 10

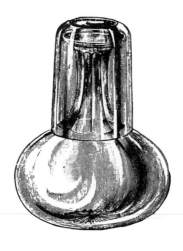

MANGELS HOUSE

570 Aptos Creek Rd., P.O. Box 302 • Aptos, California 95001
(408) 688-7982

Sitting in four acres of lawn, orchard, and woodland. Mangels House (1880s) is reminiscent of a Southern Mansion. Large rooms overlook 10,000 acres of redwood park and trails. Enjoy British hospitality in this beautiful historic country retreat.

Breakfast Cake

⅓ c. sugar
1 stick butter
1 egg
1 c. flour plus ¼ tsp. salt
1 tsp. baking powder
1 lemon grated
6 apricots or plums
¼ c. sugar
1 orange grated

Cream sugar and butter. Blend in egg. Add flour, salt, baking powder and grated lemon. Cut apricots in half and pit them. Put batter in 9" square cake tin. Press fruit halves lightly into batter, skin side up. Sprinkle batter and fruit with sugar and grated orange peel. Bake at 350° for 40 to 45 minutes.

Serves 9-12

Piperade

3-4 c. onions, thinly sliced
Bell peppers (red and green), thinly sliced
1 large clove of garlic, minced
6 medium tomatoes (peeled and seeded) cut in strips
Salt
Pepper
Basil
1 packet Pepperidge Farm puff pastry patty shells
8 eggs

Saute onions and peppers until tender. Add garlic and tomatoes. Season with salt, pepper, and basil. Boil uncovered until juices are almost gone. Add a dash of hot pepper. Cook 8 patty shells according to directions on packet. Scramble eggs. Remove cap from patty shell and soft interior. Scoop in egg and top with pepper mixture.

Serves 8

Puffed Pancake with Apple

7 eggs
2 c. milk
1¼ c. flour
3¾ tbsp. granulated sugar
1¼ tsp. vanilla
½ tsp. salt
¼ tsp. cinnamon
1¼ sticks butter
2½ apples, peeled and sliced (Granny Smith preferably)
4 tbsp. brown sugar
Sausages, cooked

Preheat oven to 425°. Use two 9½" diameter quiche dishes. In blender mix eggs, milk, flour, granulated sugar, vanilla, salt, and cinnamon. (If using a mixer, batter will remain lumpy.) Melt butter in quiche dishes in oven. Add apples. Return to oven until butter sizzles, but don't brown. Pour batter over apples in the two dishes. Sprinkle with brown sugar. Bake in middle of oven for 20 minutes until puffed and brown. Serve immediately with sausages.

Serves 10-12

---

615 Mill Street • Half Moon Bay, California 94019
(415) 726-9794

Relax and be pampered in a romantic retreat by the sea. Flower filled rooms, fireplaces, private baths overlook an English country garden with jacuzzi spa. Complimentary sherry and hors d'oeuvres, a sumptuous three-tray champagne breakfast make a luxurious escape irresistably close.

Easy Strawberry Palmiers

1 pkg. puff pastry (Pepperidge Farm)
Whipped cream
Strawberries
Sugar

Dust board lightly with sugar. Roll out pastry 6"x10", trim edges. Fold the long sides of the pastry so they meet edge to edge in the middle. Fold over again so there are 4 layers. Cut into ½" slices, brush one side with water and sprinkle sugar. Refrigerate 10 minutes. Open ends to form a "U" shape. Put on lightly greased cookie sheet, sugar side up, and bake at 425° for 15 minutes. In the middle of cooking time, turn over to brown other side. (If oven runs hot, cook at 400°.) Cool and with pastry tube, flute whipped cream in center. Top with large strawberry or serve plain and top with Homemade Ollalieberry Jam (recipe follows).

Ollalieberry Jam

1 pkg. dry pectin
6 c. crushed berries
8½ c. sugar

Add pectin to fruit in large stainless steel stock pot. Cook in place over high heat. Bring to boil, stirring constantly until mixture comes to a full boil. Add sugar. Mix well. Continue stirring, then boil hard for 4 minutes. Place in sterilized Ball canning jars. Seal with ¼" melted wax and set out overnight. In the morning, tighten jar lids. NOTE: This recipe calls for less fruit and more sugar and a little more time to cook the fruit down.

Egg Casserole

10 eggs
½ c. melted butter
1 lb. grated Monterey jack cheese
1 pt. cottage cheese
½ c. flour
1 tsp. baking powder
½ tsp. Spike (or salt)
2 4 oz. cans Ortega chopped chilies
1 4 oz. can sliced olives (zucchini, spinach, mushrooms
    optional)

Beat eggs, then beat in the next 6 ingredients. Add the chiles and olives. Grease 9"x12" baking dish, fold in prepared ingredients. Bake at 350° for 35 minutes or until knife comes out clean. May be prepared the night before and warmed up for breakfast. Serve with homemade salsa and cottage bacon slices and garnish with fresh herbs, nasturtium blossoms, cherry tomatoes, avocados or orange slices.

Serves 10-12

NEW DAVENPORT

Hwy. One • Davenport, California 95017
(408) 425-1818

Ocean hideaway nine miles north of Santa Cruz. Twelve colorful rooms decorated with antiques, handcrafts and ethnic treasures. Private baths. Artist/Owners. Wonderful restaurant and store. Friendly informal atmosphere. Beach access.

Homemade Walnut Granola

¾ c. oil
1¼ c. honey
2 tbsp. vanilla
1½ c. bran
½ c. whole wheat flour
8 c. oats
1 tsp. salt
2 tsp. cinnamon
1 c. brown sesame seeds
3 c. chopped walnuts
2 c. shredded coconut
2 c. raw sunflower seeds
2 c. raisins

Mix first three ingredients together. Mix all dry ingredients together in a large bowl. Pour honey mixture over dry mixture and blend well. Spread on a large sheet pan or 2 small cookie sheets. Bake in a 350° oven for 45-60 minutes. Stir every 15 minutes. When golden brown remove from oven. Add raisins after mixture has cooled. Store in airtight jars. Serve with fresh fruit and milk.

Aunt Austrid's Pound Cake

1 lb. butter or margarine
1 lb. pkg. powdered sugar
6 eggs
1 tsp. vanilla
1 lb. cake flour

Cream butter at room temperature. Add powdered sugar gradually and mix well. Add eggs, one at a time, mix well. Add vanilla, mix well. Add flour a little at a time. Grease and flour 2 loaf pans. Bake at 325° for 1½ hours.

EASY • FAST • YUMMY

Serves 20

5086 San Gregorio Road • San Gregorio, California 94074
(415) 747-0810

Rancho San Gregorio, a Spanish mission style house on 15 acres of rolling wooded hills, overlooks the historic coastal valley of San Gregorio. Only 45 miles from San Francisco, this picturesque retreat provides an escape to peace, serenity and a friendly country lifestyle.

Sour Cream Cinnamon Swirl

¼ lb. butter
1 c. sugar
2 eggs
2 c. flour
1 tsp. baking powder
1 tsp. baking soda
¼ tsp. salt
1 c. sour cream
1 tsp. almond extract

TOPPING:

½ c. sugar
2 tsp. cinnamon
1 c. chopped nuts

Cream butter and sugar together. Add eggs. Sift flour, baking powder, baking soda and salt and alternate with sour cream, adding to creamed mixture. Add almond extract. In a separate bowl, mix topping of sugar, cinnamon, and chopped nuts. Pour half of batter into greased tube pan. Sprinkle half of topping over it. Add rest of batter and sprinkle remaining topping over it. Swirl batter with knife. Bake at 350° for 45-60 minutes.

Serves 8-10

Rancho Spanish Souffle

1 small loaf day old French bread
4 c. milk
6-8 eggs
1 lb. pkg. bulk pork sausage
1 can diced chiles (4 oz.)
1 c. grated cheddar cheese
1 c. grated jack cheese

Layer one inch slices of French bread in a greased 10x12 Corning pan. Measure milk. Add eggs to milk and beat to mix. Pour mixture over bread, cover with foil and place overnight in refrigerator. On the following morning brown the sausage and sprinkle pieces over egg soaked bread. Add chiles and grated cheeses. Turn bread over with a fork so all ingredients are distributed throughout. Cover with foil and bake 30 minutes at 350°. Uncover and bake 30 minutes longer or until evenly browned and puffy. Serve with salsa if desired.

Serves 6-8

SEVEN GABLES INN

555 Ocean View Boulevard • Pacific Grove, California 93950
(408) 372-4341

*Splendid Victorian on the very edge of Monterey Bay. Elegantly
furnished throughout with fine antique furnishings. All rooms have
views of the ocean and all have private baths. Our sit-down breakfasts
and afternoon teas are served in the grand dining room. No smoking.
Close to the Aquarium, Cannery Row, 17-mile drive, Carmel, and
more!*

255

Mincemeat Apple Muffins

2 c. flour
2 tsp. baking powder
½ tsp. baking soda
1 tsp. salt
1 tsp. cinnamon
½ tsp. nutmeg
¼ tsp. ginger
1 c. sugar
1 c. mincemeat
½ c. milk
2 eggs
1 c. salad oil
1 medium apple, peeled, cored, and diced

Combine flour, baking powder, baking soda, salt, cinnamon, nutmeg, ginger and sugar, and mix well. Add in the mincemeat, milk, eggs, oil and apple. Mix all ingredients until just blended. Fill greased muffin tins and bake in a 350° oven for 20-25 minutes.

Yield 1 dozen

Almond Squares

¾ c. unsalted butter, softened
½ c. sugar
2 c. sifted flour
1 tbsp. grated blanched almonds
½ tsp. salt
¼ c. blanced whole almonds

Beat together butter and sugar until well blended. Add flour, grated almonds and salt. Mix until smooth. Press dough into rectangle about 14"x6"x¼" thick onto an ungreased baking sheet. Arrange whole almonds in rows on top of pressed dough. Bake in a 325° oven for about 30 minutes. Remove from oven and cut while warm into 2"x2" squares or 1"x2" diamonds.

Yields 21-30 squares

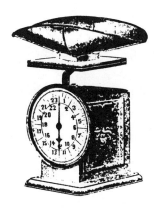

WINE COUNTRY INNS

For Information Call:
707 / 433-INNS

Sonoma County always entrances visitors with its quiet, uncommon beauty—the orchards and vineyards climbing up and down hills; the Russian River winding through redwood forests; the foggy coast, with jagged cliffs and hidden beaches. A trip to Sonoma County during any season is an enjoyable adventure.

16276 Healdsburg Avenue • Healdsburg, California 95448
(707) 433-7892

This six-acre garden retreat with separate cottages provides a perfect romantic hideaway in the heart of the Russian River Wine Valley. California country accommodations with fireplaces, whirlpool tubs for two and lovely views. Tom & Brenda Hearn, Innkeepers.

Margaret Pallardier's Fruit & Nut Cookies

1 c. shortening
2 c. sugar
2 eggs
1 tsp. cinnamon
1 tsp. nutmeg
1 tsp. baking soda
2 tbsp. sour milk
1 c. raisins
1 c. chopped dates
½ c. chopped nuts
Flour

Preheat oven to 375°. Cream shortening, sugar and eggs. Add rest of ingredients along with enough flour to make a soft dough. Place about half of the dough on well floured board, turning until enough flour has been absorbed to permit easy rolling but not stiff mixture. Roll to ½ inch thick. Cut into squares and place on greased cookie sheet. Bake until lightly browned (about 10 to 12 minutes). Repeat with second half of dough.

Yields 3½ dozen

Cheese Chili Cubes

8 eggs
½ c. flour
1 tsp. baking powder
¾ tsp. salt
3 c. shredded Jack cheese (or part cheddar/part Jack)
1½ c. cottage cheese
2 4-oz. cans chopped mild peppers

Beat eggs in mixer for 4 to 5 minutes. Add dry ingredients, mix well. Fold in cheeses and peppers. Turn into greased 9x9x2 baking dish. Bake 40 minutes at 350°. Let stand 10 minutes. Cut into sixteen squares.

Serves 8

Wedding Cookies

½ lb. butter
½ c. sugar
2 c. flour
1 tsp. vanilla
1 c. chopped nuts

Mix ingredients together and chill. Drop or roll into balls on dull side of aluminum foil lined cookie sheet. Bake about 30 minutes at 300°. Roll in powdered sugar while still warm.

Yields 3 dozen

211 North Street • Healdsburg, California 95448
(707) 433-8182

Elegant Italianate Victorian townhouse built in 1869. Twin marble parlor fireplaces and ornate mahogany dining room fireplace highlight many unique architectural features. Antiques fill the six large bedrooms. Four private baths. Swimming pool, continental breakfast.

Zucchini Quiche

1 prebaked 9" pie shell
⅔ c. grated Gruyere cheese
2 eggs, lightly beaten
1 c. heavy cream
Salt and pepper to taste
¼ tsp. freshly ground nutmeg
1/8 tsp. cayenne pepper
1 lb. zucchini coarsely grated and well drained

Preheat oven to 350°. On bottom of pie shell sprinkle half the cheese. Beat eggs, cream and seasonings together. Add zucchini. Pour into pie shell and top with remaining cheese. Bake 30-40 minutes. Let cool 10 minutes before servings.

Serves 8

Banana Sesame Seed Bread

2 c. granulated sugar
1 c. butter
6 ripe bananas, mashed
4 eggs, well beaten
2½ c. all-purpose flour
1 tsp. salt
2 tsp. baking soda
1 c. sesame seeds

In a large bowl cream together the sugar and butter until fluffy.
Add the mashed bananas and eggs. Sift together the flour, salt
and soda. Blend the flour mixture into the banana mixture. Add
the sesame seeds. Pour mixture into six small loaf pans (5½"x3").
Bake at 350° for 40-50 minutes.

Yields 6 small loaves

Easy Apple Tart

CRUST:
2 c. flour
¼ c. sugar
¾ c. butter
1 tsp. salt
½ tsp. baking powder
¼ lb. butter
½ c. finely chopped walnuts

FILLING:
2 large apples, peeled and grated
1 tbsp. apple brandy
¼ tsp. cardamom

TOPPING:
1 c. sour cream
1 egg
3 tbsp. sugar

Sift together dry ingredients. Cut in butter until mixture resembles coarse meal. Add nuts. Press into bottom and sides of a 10" tart pan. Bake at 350° for 8-10 minutes.

Toss grated apples with brandy and cardamom and place evenly over warm crust. Beat together sour cream, egg and sugar. Pour evenly over apples. Bake at 350° for 35 minutes or until lightly brown. Serve warm.

Serves 8-10

CAMPBELL RANCH INN

**1475 Canyon Road • Geyserville, California 95441
(707) 857-3476**

Rural setting, spectacular view, beautiful gardens, tennis courts, swimming pool, bikes. Three spacious rooms with fresh flowers, fruit, wine. Scrumptuous breakfast served on the terrace during warm weather. Mary Jane and Jerry Campbell, Innkeepers.

Chocolate Whipped Cream Cake

CAKE:
1 box Betty Crocker's Super Moist Chocolate Fudge Cake Mix
1 pint whipping cream
2 tbsp. sugar
1 tsp. vanilla

FROSTING:
1 small pkg. Nestles chocolate chips
¼ lb. butter or margarine
1 extra large egg
1 c. powdered sugar

Bake cake according to directions on package. DO NOT OVERBAKE! Cool on cooling racks. When cold, slice each layer in half horizontally to make four thin layers. Whip cream with sugar and vanilla until stiff peaks form. On a cake stand or pretty serving plate (or on waxed paper if you're going to freeze), place first layer of cake. Spread a thick layer of whipping cream to cover the layer. Repeat with all the layers but do not put whipping cream on top of the final cake layer. Frost the sides and top with chocolate frosting.

In top of double boiler over hot, not boiling water, melt chocolate chips and butter. Let cool. Then beat in one egg and one cup powdered sugar. Whip with electric beater until light and fluffy. Frost sides and top of cake. Use leftover frosting to decorate with pastry tube.

This cake freezes beautifully. If you want to make it ahead and freeze it, frost the cake but do not decorate it. Freeze the cake unwrapped until it is frozen solid. Then wrap airtight in foil. Freeze the leftover frosting in a jar. The day you serve the cake, thaw and decorate. This cake "ages" beautifully and actually tastes great 4 or 5 days after first serving. So it's great for entertaining and preparing ahead.

270

Serves 12-16

Blueberry Pie

PIE CRUST:
3 c. white flour
1½ c. Crisco
1 tsp. salt
5 tbsp. water
1 extra large egg
1 tsp. vinegar

PIE FILLING:
6 c. blueberries (or blackberries)
1 c. granulated sugar
4 tbsp. flour
¼ tsp. salt
½ tsp. nutmeg
½ tsp. cinnamon
1½ tsp. lemon juice
1½ tbsp. butter

Pie Crust: Cut in flour, shortening and salt until the size of peas. In a separate cup, whip the water, egg, and vinegar until well mixed. Pour over the flour mixture. Mix until it forms a ball. Place ⅓ of dough between two pieces of waxed paper which have been floured. Roll out and place in pie pan. Divide remaining dough in half and roll out to make two more crusts (one for the top of this pie and an extra one for your freezer!).

Preheat oven to 425°. In a large bowl, combine the blueberries, sugar, flour, salt, nutmeg, cinnamon and lemon juice. Mix well. Place in pie shell, dot with butter, and cover with pie crust. Crimp edges decoratively. Cut slits or a pretty "B" for blueberry in center of crust. Sprinkle with granulated sugar. Bake approximately 45 minutes until nicely browned. This pie freezes beautifully. Serve warm. Vanilla ice cream adds a special touch!

Country Meadow Inn

11360 Old Redwood Hwy. • Windsor, California 94592
(707) 431-1276

The peaceful elegance of a country setting is your reward at Country Meadow Inn. Our Queen Anne Victorian is situated on 6½ acres of rolling hills and meadowlands. Enjoy the serenity of the romantically furnished guest rooms, a full country breakfast, complimentary beverages, tasty treats, an abundance of fresh flowers inside and out and a feeling of welcomeness.

Country Breakfast Casserole

6 tbsp. butter
6 tbsp. flour
4 c. milk
2 tbsp. white wine
1/8 tsp. marjoram
Salt and pepper to taste
¼ c. minced parsley
3-4 drops Worcestershire Sauce
1½ lbs. link sausage
3 medium potatoes, cubed
1 dozen hard cooked eggs, quartered
1 lb. mushrooms, quartered, cooked and drained
½ lb. sharp cheddar cheese in ½" cubes
1 c. dry bread crumbs
½ c. grated cheddar cheese

Preheat oven to 325°. In a saucepan, cook together butter and flour over medium heat until bubbly (approximately 5 minutes). Beat in milk with a wire whisk and cook until thick. Stir in wine, marjoram, salt and pepper, parlsey and Worcestershire Sauce and remove from heat. Cut sausage into large pieces and brown. (You may use bulk sausage. It is just as good.) Evenly distribute potatoes, eggs, mushrooms, cheese cubes and sausage in a 9"x13" baking dish and cover with sauce. Combine bread crumbs with grated cheese and top casserole with this mixture. Bake uncovered for one hour. This may be made the day ahead covered and refrigerated and baked before serving.

Serves 10

Pancakes

4 egg yolks
4 c. flour*
4 tbsp. sugar
4 tsp. baking powder
2 tsp. baking soda
1 tsp. salt
¾ c. chopped nuts
½ c. oil
3½ c. buttermilk
4 egg whites

Separate eggs and combine yolks with flour, sugar, baking powder, soda, salt, chopped nuts, oil and buttermilk. Beat egg whites until stiff and fold into batter. Cook and enjoy!

---

*Combine whole wheat, rye, oat, brown rice and buckwheat flours, plus oat and wheat bran to equal the four cups. Serve the pancakes with freshly whipped cream and homemade strawberry or blueberry sauces.

Blueberries and Cheese Coffeecake

CINNAMON NUT TOPPING:
¼ c. all-purpose flour
⅓ c. packed brown sugar
1 tsp. cinnamon
¼ c. cold butter
½ c. chopped walnuts

CAKE:
3 c. all-purpose flour
4 tsp. baking powder
1 tsp. salt
1 c. sugar
1 tsp. freshly grated lemon peel
1 8-oz. pkg. cream cheese cut into ½" cubes
1½ c. fresh or frozen blueberries (not thawed)
3 eggs, room temperature
½ c. sour cream, room temperature
½ c. butter, melted
⅔ c. milk, room temperature

Grease a 13"x9" baking pan; set aside. Preheat oven to 350°. Prepare cinnamon nut topping. In medium bowl combine flour, brown sugar and cinnamon. Cut in butter until mixture resembles coarse crumbs. Stir in nuts. Set aside. In a large bowl, combine flour, baking powder, salt, sugar, and lemon peel. Add cream cheese and blueberries, tossing to coat with flour mixture; set aside. In a medium bowl, lightly beat eggs and sour cream. Stir in butter and milk. Stir into flour mixture only until dry ingredients are moistened. Turn into prepared pan; smooth top. Sprinkle with topping. Bake 55 to 60 minutes. Let stand 15 minutes. Cut and serve.

Serves 12-18

The Estate

13555 Highway 116 • Guerneville, California 95446
(707) 869-3313

A Sonoma County landmark guarded by towering redwoods, ten gracious rooms with private baths, queen beds, color televisions and in-room phones. Heated pool and spa. Evening turn-down and chocolates. Hearty country breakfasts.

Apple Butter

4 lbs. tart apples, quartered and cored
1 c. water
1 c. apple cider
Brown sugar as needed
2 tsp. cinnamon
1 tsp. ground cloves
½ tsp. allspice
Grated rind and juice of 2 lemons
1 c. each: raisins and chopped walnuts

Cook the apples in the liquid until soft. Pass through a food mill.
Add ½ c. brown sugar for each cup of puree. Add the spices, rind
and lemon juice and cook over very low heat until thick and dark
brown. This may take 3 to 4 hours. When the apple butter has
reached the desired color and thickness, add the raisins and
walnuts and pour into hot sterilized jars and seal tightly.

Yields 5 pints

Oeufs en Tripe
(Creamy Eggs with Sweet Onions)

2½ lbs. white onions, peeled and thinly sliced
¼ c. butter
1 dozen hard-boiled eggs
½ c. all-purpose flour
4 c. hot milk
Salt and pepper to taste

Slowly saute the onions in the butter, stirring frequently until very soft but not brown (about ½ hour). Cut the eggs into ½" slices and set aside. When the onions are soft, gradually add the flour to make a thick paste. Slowly blend in the hot milk and cook, stirring until sauce boils and thickens. Gently stir in all but 4 or 5 of the egg slices and add the salt and pepper. Spoon egg mixture onto large platter and garnish with reserved egg slices. Ideal for brunch served with crusty French bread and red wine.

Serves 8-10

Orange Madeleines

1 tbsp. plus ½ tsp. fresh orange juice
½ tsp. vanilla
1 large egg
¼ c. hot, melted butter
2 tbsp. sugar
¾ tsp. grated orange rind
¼ c. cake flour
¼ tsp. baking powder
Powdered sugar for garnish

Brush cups of madeleine tin with butter and set aside. With the metal blade of a food processor, process orange juice, vanilla and egg until fluffy (one minute). With the machine running drizzle remaining melted butter through the food chute. Without stopping, drizzle in the sugar and process another 30 seconds. Mix in the grated orange rind, flour and baking powder with 3 or 4 half-second pulses or until flour disappears. Spoon 1 heaping tbsp. of batter into each cup. Bake in a 325° oven for 12-15 minutes, until a golden rim forms on top of each cookie. Cool in pan on wire rack for 5 minutes. Turn out of pan and dust with powdered sugar.

Yields 1 dozen

BED & BREAKFAST
COUNTRY INN

321 Haydon Street • Healdsburg, California 95448
(707) 433-5228

The simple elegance of the Haydon House Queen Anne Victorian was designed for your relaxation. Vintage tubs, tree shaded grounds, a sunny veranda and luxurious linens add to the romantic atmosphere.

Sausage/Spinach Frittata

8 link sausage, cooked and drained well
3 tbsp. chopped green onion
1 c. cooked chopped spinach
½ c. grated cheddar cheese
¾ c. grated Swiss cheese
1 tsp. basil
½ tsp. Italian seasoning
Garlic salt to taste
8 beaten eggs
½ c. milk or Half & Half
3 oz. cubed cream cheese

Saute sausage until cooked. Saute chopped green onion slightly. Cook spinach until bright green. Mix sausage, onion, cheddar cheese, Swiss cheese and seasonings. Spread in bottom of greased quiche dish (10 inch). Distribute spinach on top. Beat eggs and milk together. Add cubed cream cheese. Pour over sausage mixture. Bake at 350° approximately 45 minutes or until set. Do not overcook.

Serves 8

Bran Muffins

2½ c. bran flakes
2 c. wheat germ (toasted)
1 c. lightly toasted sesame seeds
2 c. brown sugar
5 c. whole wheat flour
5 tsp. baking soda
1 tsp. salt
1 box raisins (16-oz. box)

2 tbsp. grated orange rind
4 slightly beaten eggs
1 c. honey
½ c. molasses
1 c. oil
1 qt. buttermilk
2 c. boiling water

Mix together in a very large bowl dry ingredients. In a separate bowl, mix the remaining ingredients. Add to well mixed dry ingredients. Bake in muffin tins at 350° for 20-25 minutes. Batter may be stored up to six weeks in jars in the refrigerator and used as needed.

Optional Additions: 1 cup walnuts, 1 cup coconut.

Yields several dozen

HEALDSBURG INN
on the Plaza

116 Matheson St., Box 1196 • Healdsburg, California 95448
(707) 433-6991

Restored Turn-of-the-Century Hotel. Up a wide paneled stairway, on the second floor are 8 spacious rooms individually furnished in antiques. All have private baths, claw foot tubs, lavishly supplied with thick towels, scented soaps and bubbles—even a rubber duckie! Bay windows overlook the historic plaza, air conditioned. Full breakfast with home baked goodies served on the old fashioned roof garden.

Brown Rice Raisin Muffins

⅔ c. all-purpose flour
½ c. whole wheat flour
1 tbsp. baking powder
1 tsp. salt
⅔ c. milk
2 eggs, lightly beaten
¼ c. oil
2 tbsp. honey
½ c. cooked brown rice
½ c. raisins

Preheat oven to 375°. Lightly grease 12 regular or 16 small muffin cups. Mix dry ingredients together in large bowl. In separate bowl combine milk, eggs, oil and honey and blend well. Stir in dry ingredients only enough to moisten. Blend in rice and raisins. Spoon into muffin tins and bake 20-25 minutes until lightly browned.

Yields 12-16 muffins

Orange Blossom French Toast

6 eggs
⅔ c. orange juice
⅓ c. Triple Sec
⅓ c. milk
3 tbsp. sugar
3 tbsp. vanilla
¼ tsp. salt
¼ tsp. cinnamon
Finely grated peel of 1 orange
8 ¾" slices French bread
3-4 tbsp. butter
Powdered sugar
Butter
Maple syrup 'and/or honey

Beat eggs in large bowl. Add orange juice, Triple Sec, milk, sugar, vanilla, salt, cinnamon, and peel. Dip bread in egg mixture, turning to coat all surfaces. Transfer to baking dish in single layer. Pour any remaining egg mixture over top. Cover and refrigerate over night. Melt butter in large skillet over medium high heat. Add bread in batches and cook until brown, about 8 minutes. (4 minutes each side.) Cut bread diagonally. Arrange on platter and sprinkle with powdered sugar. Serve immediately with butter and syrup or honey.

Serves 4

Deep Dish Chile Pie

¼ c. oil
1 tsp. minced fresh ginger
7 mild long green chiles, seeded
1 large onion chopped
1 garlic clove, minced
1 15-oz. can garbanzo beans, rinsed and drained
1½ tsp. ground coriander
¼ tsp. cumin
1 tsp. oregano (whole leaf)
¼ tsp. cayenne pepper
1 c. chopped black olives
1 4-oz. jar pimentos, drained and chopped
Salt and pepper
½ lb. fresh or frozen corn kernels
1 lb. sharp cheddar grated
Butter
1½ c. milk
3 eggs
½ tsp. salt
1/8 tsp. pepper
Pinch of cayenne and coriander
Cornmeal chive pastry (recipe follows)

Heat oil in large skillet over high heat. Add ginger and stir fry 30 seconds. Add chiles, onion and garlic. Stir fry 2-3 minutes. Add garbanzos, coriander, cumin, oregano, and cayenne. Stir fry 30 seconds. Remove from heat and add olives, pimento, salt and pepper. Cool slightly. Stir in corn. Drain if necessary, then stir in cheese. Preheat oven to 350°. Butter shallow 2½ quart baking dish. Combine milk, eggs, salt, pepper, cayenne, and coriander. Beat well. Spoon vegetable mixture in dish and pour egg mixture over top. Roll out pastry to about 1/8" thickness. Place over filling. Trim edges and press pastry to inside of dish to seal. Cut several slits on top to vent steam. Bake 1-1½ hours or until knife comes out clean. Serve hot or at room temperature.

Serves 10-12

Cornmeal Chive Pastry

½ c. all-purpose flour
⅔ c. yellow cornmeal
¼ c. cake flour
½ tsp. salt
½ c. plus 2 tbsp. cold, unsalted butter
½ c. (about) cold water
3 tbsp. minced chives or green onion tops

Combine dry ingredients in food processor. Chill butter, cut in small pieces and blend until mixture is like coarse cornmeal. Add liquid. Run processor until dough begins to gather together. Let dough rest. Add chives. Chill for 30 minutes. Roll out and place over chile pie. Serve with sour cream salsa and/or guacamole topping.

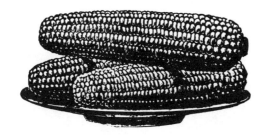

The Hidden Oak

214 East Napa
Sonoma, California
95476

A Bed & Breakfast

214 East Napa Street • Sonoma, California 95476
(707) 996-9863

One block from plaza. Completely restored old brown shingle bungalow. Antique furnished rooms, queen size beds, and private baths. Hors d'oeuvres offered each afternoon and full breakfast in the mornings. Complimentary bicycles are available.

Hidden Eggs

8 soft poached eggs
2 c. cooked spinach
6 shallots chopped
15-20 mushrooms sliced
2 tbsp. butter
2 tbsp. flour
1 c. Half & Half
Dash of chicken boullion powder
Salt and pepper to taste
½ tsp. savory
8 slices of back bacon
5 tbsp. small curd cottage cheese
5 tbsp. sour cream
5 tbsp. grated dry Jack cheese

Poach eggs and set aside. Cook spinach, squeeze out excess water. Saute shallots and mushrooms in butter. Add flour and stir until all blended. Add Half & Half to make a thick sauce. Add seasoning to taste. (Easy on the salt, as the bacon will add some.) Stir in spinach. Place one slice of bacon in the bottom of each ramekin. Place one egg on each slice. Divide spinach mixture equally over each egg. Combine cottage cheese and sour cream. Spread equally over spinach. Divide the dry Jack over top of each. Bake at 350° for 15 minutes or until cheese melts and browns and all is heated through.

NOTE: Back bacon can be replaced with regular thick slice bacon (cooked) or ham slices.

Serves 8

Buttermilk Pear Cake

½ c. margarine
1 c. white sugar
2 large eggs
2 c. whole wheat flour
½ tsp. salt
½ tsp. baking soda
2 tsp. cinnamon
½ tsp. nutmeg
½ tsp. mace
⅔ c. buttermilk
3 large pears, unpeeled and cut in small chunks
1 c. chopped walnuts

Cream margarine, add sugar and beat until all creamy and fluffy. Add eggs and beat well. Stir in dry ingredients with the buttermilk and mix well. Fold in pears and walnuts. Spread batter in a greased 8"x11" pan and bake at 350° for about 45 minutes or until a toothpick inserted in top comes out dry. Cut into 12 pieces.

Yields 12

Feta Chard Pie

2 large bunches Swiss chard (about 1½-2 lbs.)
3 tbsp. margarine
1 large onion, finely chopped
½ lb. mushrooms, finely chopped
1½ c. ham, chopped
About ½ c. fresh basil, oregano and thyme, finely chopped
Dash of pepper
8 oz. feta cheese cubed small
8 oz. cream cheese cubed small
4 large eggs beaten

Wash chard and chop stems fine. Drop in a large pot of boiling salt water. Blanch leaves a few at a time for 3 minutes. Remove with slotted spoon and drain well. Do the same with all the leaves, removing stem pieces with last leaves. Now chop the leaves coarsely. Set aside. Saute the onions and the mushrooms in the butter. Add to the chard in large bowl, along with the ham, herbs, pepper, and cheese. Beat the eggs and stir into the chard mixture. Pour into a well greased 9"x12" baking dish. Bake at 350° for 45-50 minutes. Tests done when a sharp knife inserted in the center comes out clean. Let rest 10 minutes. Cut into squares and serve.

Serves 8

21253 Geyserville Ave., Box 42 • Geyserville, California 95441
(707) 857-3356

Award-winning historic Victorian homes, beautifully restored and furnished with owners' private antique collections. Ten bedrooms, private/shared baths. Delicious breakfast. Complimentary wine. Swimming pool. Beautiful gardens. Home of Stage A Picnic Wine Tours. Bob and Rosalie Hope, Innkeepers.

Rolled Caraway Ham Slices With Cheese Sauce

DOUGH:
2 c. sifted flour
3½ tsp. baking powder
½ tsp. salt
2 tsp. sugar
½ c. shortening
2 tsp. caraway seeds
1 egg and milk to measure ⅔ c.

HAM FILLING:
2½ c. ground ham
1 medium onion, ground
2 tbsp. chopped parsley
1 tbsp. prepared horseradish
2 tsp. mustard
½ tsp. cayenne pepper
1 egg, beaten

Sift flour, baking powder, salt and sugar. Cut in shortening. Stir in caraway seeds. Add egg and milk to dry ingredients; stir until dough clings together. Knead on floured surface about 10 strokes. Roll out 12"x10" rectangle. Combine ingredients for ham filling; spread over dough. Roll as for jelly roll, starting with 12" side; cut into 8 slices. Place cut side down on ungreased baking sheet. Bake in hot oven (425°) for 20-25 minutes until light brown. Serve hot with cheese sauce (recipe follows) and garnish with parsley.

Serves 6-8

Cheese Sauce

Melt 3 tbsp. butter; blend in 3 tbsp. of flour, gradually adding 2 cups milk. Cook until thick, stirring constantly. Add 1 cup grated sharp cheddar cheese, 2 tsp. Worcestershire sauce and salt to taste. Cook until cheese melts.

Wine Country Breakfast Boboli

3-4 apples
2-3 tbsp. butter
Sugar to taste
Cinnamon to taste
Choice of cheese:
    Brie
    Cheddar
    Bleu (about 5-6 ounces)
1 Boboli cheese crust (can be purchased in the deli section of
    most major supermarkets. Comes in 2 sizes, small and
    medium)

Peel, core and slice apples. Saute peeled sliced apples in small amount of butter. Add sugar and cinnamon to taste. Thinly slice the cheese (or if using Bleu cheese, crumble it) over the Boboli crust. Add hot sauteed apple slices over cheese on top of crust. Bake in hot 400-425° oven until cheese is melted. Cut in wedges. Serve piping hot!

Variations: Other fruits can be used and instead of cheeses listed above, ricotta cheese with a small amount of sugar can be used. Especially good combination with peaches and plums.

Serves 6-8 small crust
Serves 8-10 medium crust

Piperade Basquaise

2 tbsp. olive oil
1 purple onion, chopped
2 garlic cloves, chopped
1 red and 1 green bell pepper cut into strips
4 large ripe tomatoes, peeled, seeded and chopped
Bouquet Garni (bayleaf, thyme, parsley)
Salt and pepper
½ tsp. rosemary, fresh or ¼ tsp. dried
10 eggs
½ c. butter
4-6 slices of smoked ham

SAUCE:

Heat oil in heavy saucepan, add onions and garlic and saute for 4 minutes, stirring constantly. Add peppers, saute until soft, add tomatoes, bouquet garni, salt, pepper and rosemary and simmer covered for 20 minutes. Combine eggs, salt and pepper in mixing bowl and beat until foamy. Add 2 tbsp. of butter in small pieces. Melt 4 tbsp. of butter in large skillet, pour in the eggs and stir slowly until amost set. Add the sauce and continue cooking, sprinkle with parsley and cook until set. Slide out of pan onto warm serving dish. Meanwhile, melt 2 tbsp. butter in large skillet and saute ham slices. Arrange ham on top of the eggs and serve immediately. Delicious!

Serves 4-6

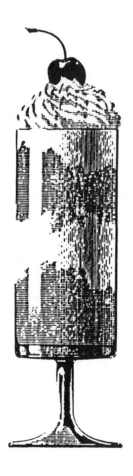

L'Auberge
du
Sans-Souci

25 West Grant Street • Healdsburg, California 95448
(707) 431-1110

A stately Victorian house nestled under spruce, cedar and redwood trees. Lovingly maintained in a French atmosphere and furnished with European antiques, queen-size beds and down comforters. The perfect place to stay on your tour of the wine country.

301

Mushroom Omelette

1½ lb. mushroom
½ cube butter
20 eggs
¼ c. water for eggs
Salt and pepper
5 cloves garlic, chopped
½ bunch parsley

Wash mushrooms in vinegar water to keep them white. Rinse well, cut in half, sliced not too thin. Saute in hot butter, medium heat, until juices are evaporated. Set aside until ready to serve. Beat eggs with water, salt and pepper. Reheat mushrooms with garlic and parsley for 5 minutes over medium heat. Heat butter on medium heat. Pour eggs in hot butter and start pushing egg mixture toward middle of pan all around. Eggs must be wet. Put mushrooms on one side and fold over. Serve immediately.

Serves 10

Scrambled Eggs with Chives

20 eggs
¼ c. milk
3 tsp. frozen chopped chives
Salt and pepper (easy on salt)
½ cube of butter

Mix first 4 ingredients. Beat well. Place butter in saute pan. Pour mixture in hot butter. When setting occurs around edge of pan, start turning and mixing them around constantly over high flame. (You must do it fast.) When eggs are lumpy and WET, they are ready. Serve immediately on hot plates.

Serves 10

Bread Pudding

12 slices stale French bread
2½ c. water plus 2 oz.
12 oz. evaporated milk
1½ c. of sugar
Pinch of salt
1 tsp. vanilla extract
⅔ c. golden seedless raisins
1 can (17 oz.) fruit cocktail, drained
1 c. flaked coconut
½ c. butter (1 cube) melted
6 eggs

Preheat oven to 350°. In large bowl, soak bread in milk, water, sugar and vanilla. Let stand 1 hour, stirring occasionally. Grease a 13"x9" baking dish with soft butter. Add to bread mixture, raisins, fruit cocktail, coconut and melted butter. Beat eggs well and add to mixture, blending well. Pour into buttered baking dish. Bake 1 hour.

Serves 12

Madrona Manor

1001 Westside Road, Box 818 • Healdsburg, California 95448
(707) 433-4231

1881 mansion on eight acres in wine country. 16 rooms, all private baths. Air-conditioned. Swimming pool. Award-winning restaurant serves California cuisine.

Caccio-cavallo (Fried Cheese)

4 oz. of Caccio-cavallo cheese*
4 tbsp. olive oil (virgin)
1 tsp. garlic, minced
1 tbsp. vinegar
1 tsp. chopped parsley
1 tsp. oregano

Cut cheese in ½" cubes and place in small skillet with olive oil and garlic. Heat over medium hot flame, add vinegar, garnish with parsley and oregano. Serve immediately accompanied with French bread. This dish sizzles when the vinegar hits the hot oil and should be served sizzling to the table.

---

*Available from ITL Foods in San Francisco.

Serves 2

Baked Semolina Gnocchi

1 qt. of milk
1 heaping c. of semolina (Avoid quick-cooking breakfast farina)
1 c. freshly grated Parmesan cheese, in units of ⅔ c. and ⅓ c.
2 tsp. salt
2 egg yolks
7 tbsp. butter, in units of 2 tbsp. and 5 tbsp.

Heat milk to just short of boiling, slowly and steadily beat in semolina, cooking until a firm mass is formed (about 10 minutes). Add ⅔ c. cheese, salt, egg yolks and 2 tbsp. of butter. Moisten a formica or marble surface with water and spread to thickness of 3/8 inch. Let cool 30-40 minutes. With a 1½ inch biscuit cutter cut the mixture into disks, moistening the tool in cold water. Smear bottom of bake and serve dish with butter. Lift the pieces of semolina which are not circles and place on bottom layer. Dot with butter and sprinkle with cheese. Over this arrange all the disks in a single layer, overlapping like roof tiles. Dot with butter and remaining cheese. This can be done early in the day. When ready to cook, heat oven to 450°, place dish in oven for 15 minutes until a light golden crust has formed. Can be prepared two days ahead and refrigerated if covered with plastic wrap.

Serves 4-6

Parmesan Eggs

2 tbsp. butter
2 tbsp. dry sherry
2 eggs
Salt and pepper
2 tbsp. Parmesan cheese

Brown butter in skillet; add sherry. Bring to boil, break eggs into mixture. Season with salt and pepper. When egg whites begin to set, remove skillet from heat. Sprinkle with cheese. Place skillet under broiler and brown cheese. (Cheese browns quickly so watch closely.)

Has a flavor of mushrooms but not a mushroom in sight!

Serves 1

5850 Melita Road • Santa Rosa, California 95405
(707) 538-7712

A turn-of-the-century railroad station restored to a country inn. The rooms are furnished with antiques. Folk art hand-stenciling in each room. Surrounded by two parks, hiking and bicycling are at your doorstep. Private baths, breakfast, wine.

Spinach Pie

2 slices bacon chopped
½ chopped onion
1 garlic clove minced
A handful of mushrooms, sliced
1 pkg. frozen chopped spinach, thawed
1½ c. milk
1 c. flour
4 eggs
Salt, hot pepper, Worcestershire Sauce and garlic to taste
1½ c. grated Jack cheese

Saute bacon, add onion and garlic and mushrooms and cook a few minutes. Mix in spinach. Whisk milk, flour, eggs and seasonings. Put spinach mixture in 12" pie plate. Top with cheese and then pour milk mixture over. Bake in 375° oven about 40 minutes or until lightly brown and puffed.

Mint Frittata with Red Peppers

3 or 4 white potatoes
½ chopped onion
2 tbsp. safflower oil
2 tbsp. butter
8 eggs, lightly beaten
4 tbsp. fresh chopped mint leaves or basil
½ tsp. salt
Pepper to taste
3 red peppers
Olive oil
Lemon or lime peel

Boil potatoes until medium tender and slice. Saute potatoes and onion in oil until they start to brown. Add butter to potatoes, and when it's bubbly, pour in eggs to which mint and seasonings have been added. Stir slightly until mixture begins to set. Then put in 500° oven several minutes until it puffs and begins to brown. Roast red sweet peppers in the broiler until they turn black. Allow to cool 15 minutes in brown paper bag with end rolled shut. Peel, seed, cut into strips. Cover with olive oil. To garnish, add grated lemon or lime peel and refrigerate. Serve with frittata.

Fig Conserve

1 lemon
1 pint small ripe figs, trimmed
1 c. sugar
⅓ c. chopped walnuts

Chop lemon coarsely in a food processor or chopper. Place figs and lemon in a saucepan. Add sugar and boil until thick. Stir in walnuts and cool. Keep in refrigerator or pour into sterilized jars and seal. Serve with spinach pie or mint frittata.

Yields 1 ½ pints

312

Pygmalion House
BED & BREAKFAST

331 Orange Street • Santa Rosa, California 95401
(707) 526-3407

Victorian, private baths, fireplace and parlor. Full breakfast, wine and cheese. One hour north of San Francisco, walking distance to the Railroad Square and Santa Rosa Plaza. Hwy. 101 and 12 intersect. Near wineries, coastline, ballooning, and Russian River area.

Ann's Bran Muffins

1 box (20 oz.) raisin bran
3 c. sugar
5 tsp. soda
3 c. white flour
1 c. wholewheat flour
1 c. uncooked oatmeal
2 tsp. salt
2 tsp. cinnamon
2 tsp. nutmeg
1 tsp. dry ginger
1 c. chopped nuts
1 c. chopped dates
1 c. currants
4 eggs
1 qt. buttermilk
1 c. cooking oil

Mix raisin bran, sugar, soda, flours, oatmeal, salt, cinnamon, nutmeg, ginger, walnuts, dates and currants in a LARGE container. Beat eggs, blend with buttermilk and oil. Pour into dry ingredients and mix well. Store covered in airtight container in refrigerator. Will keep for six weeks. Fill well greased muffin cups ⅔ full and bake at 400° for 20 minutes.

Yields 18

Fruitee Muffins

1 c. white flour
1 c. whole wheat flour
⅓ c. sugar
2 tsp. baking powder
1 tsp. cinnamon
½ tsp. salt
1 c. chopped dates
1 c. chopped nuts
2 large ripe bananas
2 eggs
¼ c. cherry yogurt
¼ c. cooking oil

CINNAMON/SUGAR TOPPING:
¼ c. sugar
1 tbsp. cinnamon

Combine flours, sugar, baking powder, cinnamon, salt, dates and nuts. Puree banana in blender to make 1 cup, blend in eggs, yogurt and oil. Combine wet and dry ingredients and blend lightly only until moistened. Fill well greased muffin tins, sprinkle with cinnamon/sugar topping and bake at 400° for 20 minutes.

Yields 18

Wonderful Walnut Coffee Cake

2 c. flour (Wondra)
1 tsp. baking powder
1 tsp. baking soda
½ tsp. salt
1 c. butter
1 c. sugar
2 eggs
2 tsp. vanilla
1 c. sour cream

TOPPING MIX:
¼ c. white sugar
⅓ c. brown sugar
1 tbsp. cinnamon
1 c. chopped walnuts

Sift flour with baking powder, soda and salt. Cream butter with sugar. Add eggs and vanilla. Mix thoroughly and blend in dry ingredients with sour cream. Spread ½ of batter in 9"x13" floured and greased pan. Spread ⅔ of the topping mix over the batter and cover with remaining ½ of the batter. Sprinkle ⅓ of the topping mix on top of batter, bake at 350° for 30 minutes or until tests done.

Serves 15-18

Ridenhour
Ranch House Inn

1250 River Road • Guerneville, California 95446
(707) 887-1033

Country-style bed and breakfast inn. Seven bedrooms individually decorated with antiques, quilts, flowers. Hot tub. Walk to river. Mr. and Mrs. R. Satterthwaite, Innkeepers.

Gravenstein Apple Crumble

6-8 Gravenstein apples
⅓ c. currants (if desired)
1 c. brown sugar
⅔ c. butter
1 c. flour
⅓ c. finely chopped walnuts
¼ c. Quaker oats

Butter a baking dish 8"x8"x2" and fill nearly to top with sliced apples and currants. Work sugar, butter, flour, walnuts and Quaker oats together until mixture is crumbly and then spread over apples. Bake 15 minutes at 400° and 25 minutes at 325° to finish. Serve with a pitcher of cream to pour over, if desired.

Serves 8

Rancho Bread

¼ c. vegetable oil
½ c. finely minced onion
⅓ c. chopped fresh Anaheim chile
1 egg, lightly beaten
2 tbsp. honey
1 c. milk
1 c. unbleached white flour
1 c. yellow corn meal (not polenta)
3 tsp. baking powder
½ tsp. salt
1 c. fresh or frozen corn, petite style
½ c. plus ⅓ c. grated sharp cheddar cheese

Heat oil in small skillet. Add onion and chiles and saute over medium heat 5-8 minutes or until onion is soft. Beat together egg, honey and milk. Combine together thoroughly flour, cornmeal, baking powder, and salt. Combine milk mixture and cornmeal mixture. Mix until well blended. Add corn, chopped sauteed chiles and onions. (Be sure to scrape in all the excess oil from the pan.) Add the ½ c. grated cheese and mix well. Spread into greased 8-inch square baking pan. Sprinkle top with the ⅓ c. grated cheese. Bake at 375° for 25-30 minutes. Serve warm with butter.

Serves 6-8

Vintage Towers Inn

302 North Main Street • Cloverdale, California 95425
(707) 894-4535

Grand Queen Anne Victorian mansion in quiet wine country town. Eight guest rooms, including three tower suites. Private baths, full breakfasts, central heat and air conditioning. A peaceful retreat at moderate rates.

Oatmeal Pancakes

4 c. rolled oats
4 c. buttermilk
7 eggs (beaten)
¼ c. sugar
½ c. shortening (melted)
1 c. (scant) all-purpose flour
2 tsp. baking powder
2 tsp. baking soda
2 tsp. salt

Night Before: Stir oatmeal and buttermilk together in a bowl. Cover. Let stand overnight out on counter.

Next Morning: Add eggs, sugar and melted shortening. Stir well to combine. Sift flour, baking powder, soda and salt into oatmeal mixture. Stir until just combined. Cook on a lightly greased hot griddle until bubbles appear and underside is golden brown. Turn once. Serve with Brandy Apple Topping. (Recipe follows.)

Serves 8

Brandy Apple Topping

¼ c. melted butter
2 tbsp. brandy
1 c. golden raisins
1 c. maple syrup
½ tsp. cinnamon
½ tsp. nutmeg
2 12-oz. cans apple pie filling
1 c. walnuts, roasted, skinned and chopped

Heat all ingredients together. Thin with small amounts of water if necessary. Serve over oatmeal pancakes.

Serves 8

Ye Olde Shelford House

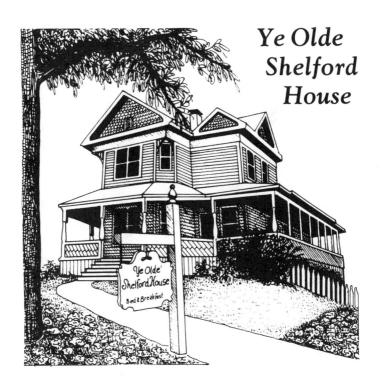

29955 River Road • Cloverdale, California 95425
(707) 894-5956

Country Victorian overlooking vineyards, full gourmet breakfast, beautifully wallpapered rooms that are light and airy, crisp and clean, and full of authentic family antiques. Sundeck and hot tub, bicycles, refreshments. Surry rides to wineries. No smoking.

Seafood Quiche

½ Onion (chopped)
2 tbsp. butter
3 beaten eggs
¾ c. light cream
¾ c. milk
½ tsp. salt
½ tsp. lemon peel
Nutmeg
7 oz. crab or shrimp
1 tbsp. flour
1½ c. Swiss cheese (grated)
¼ c. almonds (sliced)

PIE CRUST:
1 c. flour
½ tsp. salt
1½ tbsp. water
¼ oil

Saute chopped onion in butter. In a bowl mix together eggs, cream, milk, salt, lemon peel, nutmeg, seafood, flour, grated cheese. Put quiche ingredients in an oiled pie shell, top with sliced almonds. **Pie Crust:** Mix and roll out between two pieces of waxed paper. Place aluminum foil on top of pie crust and weight down with beans. Bake at 400° for 12 minutes. Remove aluminum foil and beans. Add quiche ingredients to crust and bake at 350° for 45 minutes.

Serves 6-8

Scotch Shortbread

4 c. flour
1 lb. butter
1 c. sugar

Knead above mixture in a large bowl. When thoroughly mixed put on cookie sheet (with 4 sides). Pat it evenly on sheet, then take a fork and prick holes evenly in rows over entire mixture. Bake at 250° for 1 hour or until it begins to get light brown around the edges. Cut in 1½" squares immediately. Let cool and sprinkle sugar over top.

Orange Marmalade Muffins

2 c. flour
2½ tsp. baking powder
⅓ c. sugar
¾ tsp. salt
⅓ c. salad oil
1 6-oz. can frozen orange juice concentrate thawed
1 egg
½ c. orange marmalade
½ c. nuts
Sugar

Combine in large bowl first four ingredients. Set aside. Combine next 5 ingredients and add to dry mixture. Sprinkle sugar over before baking. Bake for 20 minutes at 400°.

Serves 6-8

Index

A

B

332

Q

R

S

About the Author

Sonnie Imes, a native of Philadelphia, Pennsylvania, has lived in Incline Village, Nevada on the North Shore of Lake Tahoe for the past nine years. Her interest in cooking began when she was tall enough to reach the sink and clean up her own dishes.

Sonnie considered her dad her best critic and audience—always willing to try her new concoctions. She has even been able to transform her husband, Dick Imes' palate into a gourmet one, even though he is a confirmed meat and potatoes man.

A gourmet cook in her own right, this is her seventh book, five featuring favorite recipes of renowned restaurants in the Lake Tahoe Basin, Reno and Marin. The sixth book, *The Tastes of California Wine Country—Napa/Sonoma*, is a restaurant guide and Bed and Breakfast guide, as well as recipes from those establishments.

Sonnie has always been an innovator. Twelve years ago while living in Las Vegas, Nevada, she wrote an article for the *Nevada Times* on a dare. The article was such a success that it became a regular feature column until she left the area.

In the works now are several other cookbooks, including *The Tastes of California Wine Country—North Coast* (due to be released April 1987), *The Tastes of California Wine Country—Central Coast*, *The Tastes of Hawaii* and possibly *The Tastes of New England*.

Cookbook Naming Contest

The naming of this book was accomplished through a contest among the participating innkeepers. The prize for being chosen was a full page description of the winning inn. Over 85 entries were submitted. The two winning inns each submitted the title, *Cooking INN Style*.

The winning Inns are:

    THE BRIGGS HOUSE, Leslie Hopper, Manager
    Sacramento

    FOOTHILL HOUSE, Sue Clow, Innkeeper
    Calistoga

Additional information about these inns appears on the following pages.

Foothill House

3037 FOOTHILL BOULEVARD
CALISTOGA, CALIFORNIA 94515
(707) 942-6933

"Foothill House is definitely special."

Bed & Breakfast
Homes Directory
by Diane Knight

"(The) Evergreen Suite of Foothill House in Calistoga is among the most romantic in the area."

Chicago Tribune
by Carolyn McGuire

"Foothill House. . . is the best bed-and-breakfast place in the world."

Western Living Magazine
by Jurgen Gothe

". . . Innkeepers Michael and Susan Clow offer their guests a very special brand of hospitality. . ."

Bed & Breakfast American Style
by Norman T. Simpson

"Best B&B place to stay. Foothill House in Calistoga is friendly, tastefully appointed and comfortable."

Wine on the Table
William Clifford,
syndicated columnist

Foothill House is nestled among the western foothills just north of Calistoga. The natural country setting is distinguished by the wide variety of lovely old trees that surround it keeping it comfortably shaded and cool. The inn offers views across the valley of wooded hills and Mount St. Helena. Being in the foothills, nature abounds with such wildlife as quail, hummingbirds and hawks.

Three cozy, yet spacious suites are individually decorated with country antiques. The color scheme for each room is centered around the handmade quilt which adorns the queen-size four-poster bed. All rooms have a private bath and entrance, a small refrigerator stocked with complimentary wine and mineral water, a fireplace for added warmth and ambience in winter. Air-conditioning and ceiling fans add to your summer comfort.

A generous continental breakfast features fresh fruit, homemade breads and muffins and freshly squeezed orange juice. Guests may partake in the Sunroom, outside on the terrace, or in the privacy of their room. In the late afternoon guests relax during "wine appreciation hour" with complimentary wine and cheese.

Foothill House is in close proximity to every attraction the Napa Valley has to offer. The innkeepers, Susan and Michael Clow act as the guests' personal concierge to insure a memorable stay in the Napa Valley.

The Briggs House
A Bed & Breakfast Inn

This vintage valley turn-of-the-century home has all the best features of an old friend: steps up the front and back to elicit respect, warm wood floors and furnishings to make one feel welcome, open stairwell to encourage communication, memorabilia to dream of by-gone days, and comfortable hospitality to make one wish for many returns.

Breakfast at Briggs is a total delight—from the aroma of fresh baked muffins in the evening to the last savored taste of the morning's specialty. The morning meal might be enjoyed in the garden amidst the camellia or orange blossoms, on warmer days, or by a crackling fire in the parlor when there's a chill in the air.

In the evening, one might enjoy a rock on the front porch swing or garden hammock, a sunset bicycle tour of the capitol or Sutter's Fort, a stroll to any one of a number of fine local restaurants for dinner or dessert, or just a snuggle by the fire with a good book or unhurried conversation.

Come and enjoy the friendship of the Briggs House!

NOTES

THE TASTES OF TAHOE

The Tastes of Tahoe
P.O. Box 6114
Incline Village, NV 89450

Please send _____ copies of **The Tastes of Tahoe I** at $6.95 each.

Please send _____ copies of **The Tastes of Tahoe II** at $7.95 each.

Please send _____ copies of **The Tastes of Tahoe III** at $7.95 each.

Please send _____ copies of **The Tastes of Reno** at $6.95 each.

Please send _____ copies of **The Tastes of Marin** at $7.95 each.

Please send _____ copies of **The Tastes of California Wine Country - Napa/Sonoma** at $9.95 each.

Please send _____ copies of **Cooking INN Style** at $9.95 each.

Please send _____ copies of **The Tastes of California Wine Country - North Coast** at $9.95 each.

Add $1.50 postage and handling for the first book ordered and .50¢ for each additional book.

Enclosed is my check for _____

Name _____

Address _____

City _____ State _____ Zip _____

☐ This is a gift. Send directly to:

Name _____

Address _____

City _____ State _____ Zip _____

☐ Autographed by the author.

Autographed to: _____

NOTES

NOTES

NOTES

NOTES

NOTES

NOTES

NOTES